The Oasis Sisters

Royal Caribbean's Fleet of the
World's Biggest Cruise Ships

PAUL CURTIS

COVER

This artist impression of the five sisters meeting at sea like shown is yet to happen. If it ever does, it will have the five captains on full alert!

Copyright © 2019 Paul Curtis
THE OASIS SISTERS
Royal Caribbean's Fleet of the World's Biggest Cruise Ships
2nd edition

All rights reserved. Without limiting the rights under copyright above, no part of this publication may be produced, stored or introduced into a retrieval system, or transmitted in any form or by any means (electronic, mechanical, photocopying, recording or otherwise) without the prior written permission of both the copyright owner and the publisher.

DEDICATION

This book is dedicated to Jarvis, Byron, Holly and ship lovers everywhere.

Contents

Phoenix Rising	9
Creating the Unthinkable	27
Building the Dream	57
Powering the Behemoths	65
The Maiden Voyage	75
Anchors Aweigh	87
Food, Food, Glorious Food	99
Pieces of Eight	109
RCL Ships Round-Up	115
About the Author	128

Harmony of the Seas making her maiden arrival at Southampton England.

Chapter One

Phoenix Rising

Hey, Hey It's the Sixties. The race to be first to the moon is on. JFK is swiveling on his Oval Office chair, the Beatles are singing 'Yeah, yeah, yeah' and a whole new wave of excitement and fashion is sweeping the western world. Just the time, one might think, to start dreaming of building huge new passenger ships of a size and wonder never seen before.

However, for shipping companies it was quite the reverse. For them, the only Swinging Sixties they could see was the noose dangling over their office doorways. Jet travel and the airlines were taking over and offering ever decreasing air fares. This hit the passenger lists of the Transatlantic liners very hard and with the introduction of faster and bigger jets, more and more people, wishing to journey from one country to another, were ignoring the ships and opting to go by plane.

Unbelievably, the British Union of Seamen chose this very time to mount their infamous strike of May 1966. As British ships arrived back in England, the union's 62,500 members walked off in pursuit of what ship owners described as a seventeen percent increase in pay. As a result, Southampton became a ship spotter's paradise with long rows of famous ships from Union Castle, P&O, Shaw Savill and the like, lining the docks: stranded, forlorn and empty. There we so many ships tied up in port in that some had to be moored three abreast. Few of the ships ever sailed again under the British Red Ensign.

With passenger shipping no longer a viable business proposition, the companies tried to sell them off. The long serving, giant post war rulers of the seas, such as Cunard's *Queen Mary and Queen Elizabeth*, French Line's *France* and the United States Line's *United States* and *America*, were all sinking under the auctioneer's hammer.

This disaster was not confined to just Southampton. Shipping piers around the world were looking like a massive Macy's clearance sale. Passenger ship companies and builders were going broke and the surviving ships were scrambling to convert from passage-making to full-time cruising.

Media and travel pundits were proclaiming the era of building big ships was over: finished, kaput, gone forever: deader than the proverbial dodo.

But one shipping company was to prove these pundits wrong.

Whilst the writing was on the wall for liners that carried passengers across the world from port A to port B, the idea of smaller ships pottering around tourist spots was gaining popularity. The concept of just cruising around some islands for a vacation began as early as the 1850's, but only a few travelers could afford such a frivolous novelty. However, over the years, living standards changed and the appeal grew.

To take advantage of this, more ships opted to avoid the stormy, winter Atlantic crossings by basing their ships in New York City. Sailing from here they could find new passengers wanting to cruise to the warmer smooth waters of the Caribbean. Come summer, the ships switched back to their Transatlantic trade. So the cruise business was still in its infancy and the first major boost to the United States cruise market did not come until some of the ships switched to their base from New York to Miami and began offering full time cruising schedules.

The advantage of Miami was that it could be quickly and inexpensively accessed by air from most places in America. In a matter of a few hours, the winter snow and ice of the East Coast were replaced with the sunshine and blue skies of Florida. Best of all, to reach the warm and tranquil waters of the Caribbean by flying to Miami instead of sailing from New York, passengers were spared the long, cold and often bumpy ride off Cape Hatteras.

An early arrival on the Miami cruise ship scene was a man with extraordinary vision. Edwin Stephan was a decorated Korean War officer who afterwards entered the hospitality industry as an hotelier. Using this experience, he then moved on to become a Miami based, cruise company general manager.

Edwin Stephan saw first-hand the adaption of ships to the Caribbean cruise market, but he recognized the cold reality was that these vessels were just not suited to the job they were now being tasked to do. Edwin thought that for cruising, a special design should be introduced. Conventional passenger ships had deep hulls that required more depth of water than could be found in the docks of the small Caribbean islands. So, unable to be berthed at the dockside, the ships had to anchor off and tender passengers in lifeboats across the swells in the bay to the shore.

What was really called for were ships with a shallow draft: vessels that could safely float in shallow water. He was also after lighter weight to increase speed and fuel economy. Most importantly, he wanted his ships to have a

The founders: top left: Edwin Stephan; top right: Anders Wilhelmsen; Middle left: Arnie Wilhelmsen; Middle right: Richard D Fain; Bottom: Harry Larsen of Gotaas-Larsen is on the extreme left; On the extreme right of the group are Sigurd Skaugen and Arne Wilhelmsen.

wow factor and be immediately recognizable as a special cruise ship, rather than the traditional ocean liner look.

He worked up his designs with fellow cruise expert Peter Whelpton, and then took off on the difficult mission of trying to find financial backers to bring his dream to reality. Although Edwin had an excellent reputation in the cruise industry, in the troubled financial times of the late 1960's, it wasn't easy to get financial support.

His quest for funding for his ideas took him across the United States and eventually to Europe. However, he was beginning to feel that although he was sure that he had solved the cruise ship design problem, he would never find the necessary financial support to transform his dream to reality. Appropriately enough for the cruising world, popular legend has it that the thing that allowed Edwin Stephan's idea to move from conception to birth was a ship board romance.

At this point, enter stage left, a Norwegian ship-broker based in New York. After hearing Stephan's new concepts, he was urged to take a cruise to see just how much improved the cruise experience would be.

To take time away from the office and go jaunting off on a cruise ship was a big ask for a busy businessman. But it just so happened that our investor was in love with a lady radio operator on one of the Miami cruise ships. Guess what? Yes, he agreed to take the trip. And surprise, surprise: he chose to go on his girlfriend's ship.

Fortunately, he also found the time to become totally sold on the potential of Stephan's new approach to cruise ship design. So, although Stephan's financial quest had previously taken him to the offices of Norway's shipping magnates, he returned again, but this time in company with his powerful and influential backer. And sure enough, previously closed doors were miraculously opened.

Still not everyone was receptive, but eventually everything changed at a meeting arranged with Sigurd Skaugen, a grand old man of shipping. Born in 1907, Sigurd was now well into his seventies with a highly profitable company that had been building ships for more than a hundred years.

After exhaustive questioning, Skaugen was sold on Edwin Stephan's plans. However, he was still reluctant to take the huge financial risk all on his own. He approached Anders Wilhelmsen, a fellow Norwegian shipping magnet, in a bid to share the financial burden.

The Wilhelmsen family name was also no stranger to the shipping business and had been associated right from the early days of sail. Today many tankers and freighters still bear the name and it is very much at the forefront of merchant shipping. Importantly, Anders Wilhelmsen had proved himself and his entrepreneurial skill in his own right by successfully founding his own business amidst the difficulties of the Second World War.

He also liked the concept and so it was that in 1967, when the cost of a first-class postage stamp in the United States was just five cents, Skaugen and Wilhelmsen agreed to build two ships designed to Stephan's ideas. To do this they took equal shares in a new company to be called Royal Caribbean Cruise Lines. Such was their confidence, an option for a third ship was also mooted. The orders for the first two ships were placed with the Finnish ship builders Wärtsilä. But building a cruise liner is a lengthy undertaking and it would be two years before the first of the two new ships could be delivered.

Meanwhile, Edwin Stephan was appointed as inaugural president of the fledgling cruise line. He set up a small office in Miami and began the tasks of organizing the new ships' customer operations and laying the foundations for the marketing program. It was game on.

The two ships were to be able to carry a maximum of 870 passengers, have a crew of 300, a service speed of 21 knots. In landlubber talk that's a tad over 24 miles per hour.

The first ship to arrive was the *Song of Norway*. At 18,416 gross tonnage, she was just one twelfth the size of the 225,282-gross tonnage of the *Oasis of the Seas* and the *Allure of the Seas*. They are also twice as long as *Song of Norway*. Now that's quite a difference, but then they were not to arrive until 26 ships later.

Song of Norway was a reasonable sized ship for its time and could accommodate up to 914 guests. But to continue the comparison, the Oasis class ships can carry 6,284 passengers. The *Song's* staterooms numbered 377 against the Oasis class 2,700 and the number of crew required to service the passengers and look after the ship went from 345 to 2166! The *Song* had one pool compared to the Oasis six, plus ten jacuzzis and two wave flow riders.

So, this gives you an immediate perspective of just how far Royal Caribbean took ship building in the forty years between 1970 and 2010. And thus, we need to make a mental adjustment, for those of us old enough, to think back to how things were in 1970.

Key to Stephan's design vision was that the new ships should have a wow factor and would immediately stand out by having a superstructure design that would readily identify them as belonging to Royal Caribbean Cruise Line.

His first idea was to add a tall space needle, reminiscent of the famous one in Seattle, on the top deck. This would be guaranteed to gather attention in any port. But at that time, this bold idea proved difficult to convert into practical marine feasibility.

Instead the designers came up with a large and striking frisbee-like cocktail lounge embodied into the funnel structure. It was a bold move: it had the look of a flying saucer and transformed the often ugliness of a ship's funnel into a striking modern feature. Thus, the Viking Crown Lounge was born and for years it was used in the company's 'Sail a Skyscraper' advertisements. And people seeing it did indeed say, 'wow!'

Under the guidance of exterior ship styling expert, Gier Grung, the new ships were given a high raked clipper bow and a large fin-shaped funnel located towards the stern. For livery, a wide and bold blue stripe was painted around the base of the superstructure and the funnel dramatically boasted the now familiar crown and anchor logo.

The whole effect resembled an airline paint job. This was a deliberate move. The idea was to seamlessly link, in the minds of passengers, their airplane arrival in Miami with the super modern ship towering over them when boarding.

While the Finnish ship yard Wärtsilä in Helsinki was busy building the first of the two ships, the fledgling company had no time to rest on its laurels. There were two main areas that had to be developed simultaneously: the running operations of the nautical side of the ship and the passenger hotel and restaurant side.

All nautical matters, such as navigation systems, propulsion and crew handling of the vessels at sea, were taken on by Sigurd Skaugen in Norway.

In 1970, the first ship arrived: the Song of Norway. Photo: © Tony Garner

Royal Caribbean began its claim to building the world's biggest cruise ships with the Song America which was launched in 1982. Photo: © Ian Donald

Meanwhile, in Miami, Edwin Stephan took responsibility for all the matters effecting passenger comforts and the cruise experience. Not surprisingly, there were occasional areas of contention between the two different sets of needs that needed to be thrashed out.

Skaugen sent to Miami an experienced former liner captain, Aage Lindstad, as the designated future captain of the first ship. His job included overseeing the recruitment and training of deck officers, engineers and seamen and liaising between matters maritime and the running of the hotel side of the ship.

While he was focused on ensuring operations met the highest standards of seamanship, Edwin Stephan wanted more. He wanted the ship's officers to comfortably mix with the passengers and enhance their cruise experience. This meant they had to learn social skills and have a good working knowledge of all things American.

In the 1960's some crusty old-salts, although always excellent on the matters relating to the nautical aspects, were not always necessarily first class in the charm department. Indeed, some gave off an air of feeling that passengers on board were a necessary inconvenience!

But Stephan succeeded in persuading Skaugen this was an important aspect of cruising and that ships' captains and officers indeed needed to train in passenger relations. Thus, they were all sent off to a 'charm boot camp' in Oslo.

At the conclusion of their course, the passing out exam for the officers was to host a dinner at the local US Embassy. Afterwards the guests attending were asked to comment on how well the officers did. Which they did, but very diplomatically of course! It was, with apologies to William Shakespeare, a case of the Taming of the Crew.

Back in Miami, a similar exercise was being conducted for potential ship's employees: such as waiters, bar staff and chefs. Mock-ups of key areas of the new ships were built in a warehouse. Here potential crew were trained in everything from quickly getting in and out of the kitchen without knocking into each other and sending plates and dinners flying, to the right and proper way to engage in conversation with the passengers. Those that failed the course, were weeded out as Skaugen and Stephan were determined that the maiden cruise would see Royal Caribbean Cruise Lines hit the deck running.

While all this was going on, the directors thought things were going so well, that they should progress the mooted idea of a third ship with the same specifications into a firm order. So, in 1968, to facilitate the financing of this, a new partner was brought in. This was the Norwegian shipping company, Gotaas-Larsen: a business co-founded in 1946 by Harry Larsen and Trygve Gotaas.

At the same time, another change on the board occurred: the 70-year-old Anders Wilhelmsen died and his seat on the board passed to his progressive and Harvard Business School educated son, Arne Wilhelmsen.

At 40 years of age, Arne was considerably younger than his fellow board members and moved to modernize company procedures. While all three of the partners were active in commercial shipping, such as freighters and tankers, they were very reliant on Stephan for his knowledge of passenger ships and cruising.

The company's first ship was delivered in 1970 and at the suggestion of Sigurd Skaugen was named Song of Norway, after the popular operetta. This set a trend with the partners each taking a turn at the honor of naming a ship.

The second ship, delivered in 1971, doubled the company's passenger capacity, and the naming rights passed to Arne Wilhelmsen who opted for Nordic Prince.

The third ship arrived in 1972 and the name chosen by Gotaas-Larsen was *Sun Viking*. As the company grew, in the cause of fleet coherency, this ad hoc way of naming ships was changed.

Such was the success of the new venture, by the end of the fourth year of operation it was obvious that *Song of Norway* was just not big enough to meet the passenger market demand. To build a new ship would take too long, so Royal Caribbean adapted an idea that its directors had seen successfully applied to cargo ships. That was to lengthen an existing ship. Although it had never been done before to a cruise ship, the Song of Norway was sent back to the shipyard to be cut in half and have a new section inserted in the middle. The reverse nip and tuck operation lengthened the ship by an extra 85 feet. That's the same as the width of the Brooklyn Bridge. The stretching operation was such a great success that the procedure was repeated on the Nordic Prince in 1980. The idea was soon being copied by other cruise ship companies.

The popularity of cruising on Royal Caribbean continued to grow at a

The Crown and Anchor logo proudly sported on the funnels of Royal Caribbean Cruise Ships.

Comparisons Between Royal Caribbean's First Ship		
Song of Norway and its 28th Ship *Allure of the Seas*		
Ship	NORWAY	ALLURE
Maiden Voyage	07-Nov-70	01-Dec-2010
First Captain	Aage Lindstad	Herman Zini
Gross Tonnage	18,416	225,282
Length	552 feet	1,187
Passengers	914	6,284
Crew	345	2166
Staterooms	377	2700
Main Dining Seating	427	2858
Pools	1	18

phenomenal pace so to meet the demand in 1982 the Song of America was launched. At just under 704 feet, 37,584 gross registered tons and carrying 1611 passengers she was more than twice the size of the first three ships.

On her launch, she became the largest ship specifically built for cruising. In fact, there were only two larger passenger ships afloat: *The QE2* and the *Norway*, which was originally named the France. But big as *Song of America* was, she was a mere minnow when compared with Royal Caribbean's future building plans.

The fact that all ships were constantly sailing with a full passenger list ensured companies operations were financially successful. However, it was not always smooth sailing in the boardroom. The directors were each individually highly successful shipping experts, but each was also used to running their own companies in their own way.

Through the eighties, Stephan often found himself in the middle of conflicting views between his directors. This was a difficult situation for Stephan as the shipping magnates had the money, but Stephan did not.

His position was made even more difficult by the fact that the constitution of the company required all major decisions between the three shareholders to be unanimous. And it seemed there was little they could agree on!

This caused delays to Stephan's planned expansion. Furthermore, the problem was compounded by the fact that at the end of the year the constitution required all the net profit to be distributed directly to the three shareholders, leaving the company itself with no reserves for growth. So while Stephan was all for rapid expansion, as he was not a shareholder there were often delays in ordering new ships.

Changes at Gotaas-Larsen brought in a new representative for that company to the Royal Caribbean board: Jack Seabrook. Seabrook immediately found the limitations of the current board system. To break the deadlocks occurring in the boardroom he brought in one of his own company men, Richard Fain, a graduate MBA with a history of being a successful company director.

Meanwhile, the problems in the boardroom became known and soon other cruise ship companies came sniffing around to try and stitch up take-over deals. But the company remained independent and by the 1990's had secured long term financial arrangements that would allow it to grow at its proper rate.

Seabrook and Fain turned Royal Caribbean into an ordered and functional corporation. Their first achievement had been to make Seabrook's consent to the investment in *Song of America* conditional upon a change in the company's constitution. This required that $3 million would be retained by the company before distributing the remaining earnings to the shareholders. Now the company at last, had some reserves and could start to capitalize on its popularity with potential cruise passengers.

Working well together, in 1983 Fain and Stephan succeeded in convincing board members there was potential for even further growth and got them to consider the idea of building the largest cruise ship in the world.

This would make it about twice the size of Song of America and it would be the largest passenger ship built since the *Queen Elizabeth* in 1938. For backing, Royal Caribbean and Admiral Cruises were merged with Andes Wilhelmsen. Royal Caribbean also entered into a joint ownership agreement with the Pritzer family, owners of the Hyatt Hotel Chain and the Ofer family, owners of one of the world's largest shipping companies.

Under Richard Fain's chairmanship, a special lead team was created. This consisted of representatives from the three shareholders, the heads and management of the company's operating departments and the design team from the Wärtsilä shipyard. Three separate support sub committees covered the areas of finance, marketing and technical design.

When the feasibility study had been completed, the management team resolved a detailed contract specification. Thus, the idea of the Sovereign class ships was born. The first to arrive was the *Sovereign of the Seas*. By then the *Queen Elizabeth* had been withdrawn from service so at the time of her maiden voyage on January 16, 1988, at 73,192 GT, Sovereign became the largest passenger ship. But unlike the *Queen Elizabeth*, this lady was built expressly for cruising and could carry 2744 passengers in great comfort.

Emboldened by their continuing success, the company ordered a further two ships in the same class. It also started a new naming tradition which has been followed to this day. The company decreed that all ship's names end with 'Of the Seas'.

Built by Chantiers de l'Atlantique in St. Nazaire, France with French financial backing, the *Monarch of the Seas* followed in 1990 and the *Majesty of the Seas* in 1991. These ships were destined for the ever-growing Caribbean market, but the company, seeking to continue its expansion, began casting its eyes at new regions around the world to send its ships. Today, these include Australia, the South Pacific, the Mediterranean and Northern Europe.

Rival shipping companies were also building bigger ships, but Royal Caribbean didn't just meet this challenge. Most of the time it bettered it with each of its ship launches setting a new record for being the largest passenger ship ever built.

In 1993, Royal Caribbean went public and listed on the New York Stock Exchange under the symbol RCL. In the following year, the company completed a second six story building in the port of Miami.

By 1997, the company was running as a slick well managed company with enormous prospects. To reflect its now global operation and itineraries it was renamed from Royal Caribbean Cruise Line to Royal Caribbean International.

In 1999, Royal Caribbean smashed its competitors with the introduction of the Eagle class. The lead ship was the *Voyager of the Seas* which weighed in at a whopping 137,276 tons. Carrying 3,840 passengers, she attracted huge spectator crowds at every port she visited.

In 2003, at the age of 71, Ed Stephan retired from his position as vice-chairman of the company. As a founder of Royal Caribbean across three decades he had held numerous positions, including president, CEO, vice chairman and general manager.

During his tenure, Stephan supervised the creation of a fleet of 25 cruise ships and pioneered a number of novel shipboard features that went on to become industry standards. In recognition of his great achievements, he was inducted into the Cruise Industry's Hall of Fame.

When he retired, the company was in a strong position and went on from strength to strength. Richard Fain became the chairman and chief executive officer in 1988. He developed a team which included Adam Goldstein as president and chief operating officer and Michael Bayley. Michael held a number of senior positions for a thirty-year period and in 2014 became president and CEO of Royal Caribbean International.

Today the global cruise company owns six brands: Celebrity Cruises, Royal Caribbean International, Pullmantur, Azamara Club Cruises, CDF Croisières de France, and the joint venture, TUI Cruises. Together, the parent company operates 41 ships and carries more than five million guests every year.

In 2006, it launched the Freedom class with its first ship being the *Freedom of the Seas*. Carrying 4,375 passengers, she raised the tonnage bar to 154,407. In the same year, the company announced that it was building a further two ships in the Freedom class.

But before its competitors could even draw breath from this, the company showed its testicular magnitude and went on to order a further two ships that would be 45 per cent bigger and take the new tonnage factor records way past 200,000 tons to more than 225,000!

Photo: © Paul Curtis

Balconies on Allure. Photos: © Paul Curtis

Imagine that. Not building just one unconceived mega-size of passenger ship, but two of them: one after the other! And each ship would cost the line around US $1.4 billion. Each of the two ships would be four football pitches long, wider than the wings of a Jumbo 747 jet and take up the same space as five of them lined up head to tail on a runway - not an unfamiliar sight to those flying out of Chicago!

The proposed build was named as Project Genesis and its boldness, if not sheer audacity, was truly staggering.

The first to arrive was the *Oasis of the Seas*. Launched in 2009, she weighed in at 225,282 tons and was 1,178 feet long, 213 feet wide, could carry 6,296 passengers. She immediately snatched from Freedom of the Seas the crown of being the largest passenger ship ever built.

Close on her heels and in the following year, came the *Allure of the Seas*. But, although she was conceived, specified and built as an identical ship, something had gone wrong. Both ships had an identical tonnage, but at the time of her official measuring she came in at nearly two inches longer than the Oasis!

This was not planned and was put down to metal temperature variations during the building or measuring phase. But it put the cat amongst the pigeons between the crews of the world's two largest cruise ships. Somewhat to the chagrin of the *Oasis*, *Allure* boldly laid claim to the title of being the largest cruise ship ever built!

But in turn, her reign was to be short lived. Rather than see its two sisters squabbling over the title, Royal Caribbean settled the dispute by ordering yet another ship. This was planned to be a whole two feet longer than the *Allure*. So there!

Launched in 2016, this third ship, the *Harmony* of the Seas, lifted the tonnage by 1718 gross tons. However, as both the crews of the *Allure* and the Oasis are quick to point out, she will carry a few less passengers. 'Mirror, mirror on the wall, who's the fairest of us all!'

The answer is neither, as Royal Caribbean announced a forth ship to be built in the Oasis Class. *Symphony* of the Seas. She was delivered in 2018 and, she is, of course, a bit bigger again. Amazingly the company then went on to announce a fifth ship in the Oasis class to be delivered in 2022. Just a smidge bigger again, of course. Obviously, RCL has enjoyed the publicity benefits of each time launching their new Oasis as the biggest cruise ship in the world.

On their funnels, the five largest cruise ships in the world, the near-identical mega sisters, all proudly sport the company's gold Crown and Anchor. At a

Royal Caribbean advertising heavily promotes its 'wow' concept.

cost of seven billion United States dollars, on any given day on various seas, there could be nearly 50,000 people living in a special Oasis world entirely created by the visionaries at Royal Caribbean. Yes, that thought is enough to make anyone go 'wow'.

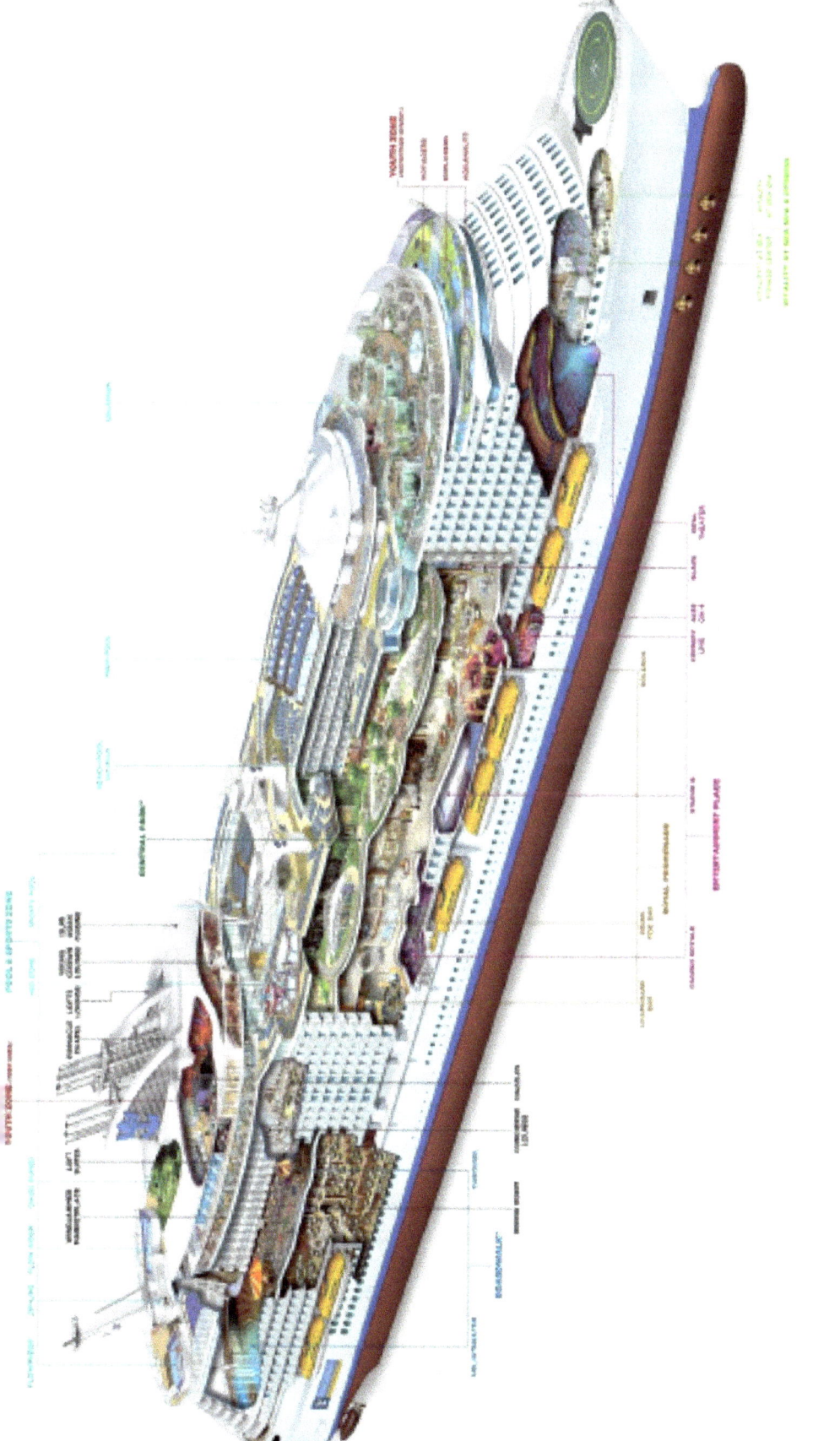

CHAPTER TWO

Creating the Unthinkable

Why on earth would you want to build the largest ship in the world? What would that mean for passengers?

True comfort on a cruise ship depends on two main factors: the passenger space ratio and the number of crew to service each individual passenger. The gross registered tonnage is a figure calculated to measure the internal volume of a ship, not its weight. So, to work out the passenger space ratio you divide the tonnage by the average number of passengers.

You can see that when you start with 225,000 tons, you have lots of room to play with. And it's the same with the crew service. You simply divide the number of crew by the number of passengers and you get an indication of the ratio of service personnel to passengers.

A new intelligent design approach and good crew training has ensured everything has been scaled up to make for maximum comfort. Proof of this is soon discovered as you embark first board the ship. Early proof of this is found when you board and when you disembark. Because everything has been so well designed and managed, these procedures on an Oasis ship are amongst the fastest of any ship. Even on the first day of boarding you can be from your taxi curbside and being shown your stateroom in fifteen minutes. Even the smallest of ships can have trouble equaling that.

There are many other benefits of being on the mega-sized Oasis class. There is the sheer variety of everything: the various neighborhood districts, the wide scope of entertainment, the different types of bars and the wide choice of restaurants. You can choose between going for a stroll in the park or sitting with a book in the peaceful privacy of your own balcony.

However, if you meet some people you want to see again, you should exchange contact details. Otherwise, you can go the whole trip and not find them! So, oddly enough, if you so desire, the vastness of the ship can make for more privacy. There is no doubt, the design team has achieved a miraculous result.

Imagine designing an entire small city, all at once. Then imagine that city not only has to float, but to cruise at upwards of twenty knots while providing the greatest vacation experience for more than 5,400 guests. And then remember this must be done for every single day of every single week. Furthermore, there could be no costly down-time for port turnarounds.

That was the challenge Royal Caribbean faced when it began planning the *Oasis of the Seas*.

The company brought together the largest creative shipping team ever assembled. It used as many as thirty-seven design firms, twenty architectural firms, one hundred and thirty members of Royal Caribbean's own New Building & Fleet Design Group and an equally large staff of architects and engineers from the builders' shipyard.

'It was a humongous project,' said Harri Kulovaara, who is the executive vice president of Maritime, Royal Caribbean and a naval architect and engineer. It was Harri's job to oversee the six-year journey of turning the Oasis idea into a mega ton reality.

'Altogether, it required between nine to ten million working hours for design and construction.'

Beginning in 2003, Royal Caribbean's New Building group began working with the shipyard's naval architecture group. For the next two years, it acted as the linchpin of a steering committee made up of senior company management, operations and marketing executives and key members of the consulting architects.

All told, this group developed and evaluated more than fifteen general configurations for what was then known as 'Project Genesis'.

It gradually honed the design into the creation of special neighborhood areas within the vessel and introduced a dramatic split-superstructure design that allowed daylight to flood right down into the center of the ship. This innovative creative concept was the idea of Harri Kulovaara.

Royal Caribbean chairman Richard Fain described the design as an evolutionary process. 'You learn from doing it on other ships, and each time you learn more, and you use that.'

Royal Caribbean' design consultants specialized in such areas as restaurant and nightclub design, theaters and entertainment venues, hotels, landscaping architecture, lighting, graphic design, art, and right down to the manufacture of classic carnival carousels.

At intensive multi-day sessions, designers would present their ideas to the steering committee of their fellow architects and designers. Everyone was encouraged to share their comments and suggestions. The objective was to

Looking down into the open center of Allure of the Seas. Photo: © Paul Curtis

ensure that all design aspects were orchestrated to create a shared overall look and feel.

'The design team has really worked to make sure everything harmonizes, but there's also a lot of serendipity here,' said Richard Fain. 'One of the problems with, say, planned communities is that it's all plain vanilla.

'What made *Oasis of the Seas* special is how well quite disparate elements fitted together. Almost anywhere you go on this ship, you're going to see places of wonder; where you turn a corner and you're surprised: because you never expected to see what you're seeing.'

The design and architecture firms involved included Atkins Global of London, England. This employs 8,000 creative staff in more than 200 offices worldwide. Under the leadership of Tom Wright, Kevin Johnson and Kate Lockey, the Atkins Global team created much of the design for the Royal Promenade, Boardwalk, Central Park, and the Rising Tide Bar.

This was the first moving bar at sea. It moves elevator-like between the Royal Promenade and Central Park. Passengers alight at Central Park beneath two huge, arched glass skylights known as the Crystal Canopies.

The open decks, the Solarium, the Solarium Bistro, the pools, sports courts, flow rider and zip line were all the work of Arkitektbyrån AB of Gothenburg in Sweden. These consultants had worked with Royal Caribbean since 1985 when they introduced the first floating mini-golf course on the *Legend of the Seas*. Under the guidance of Lars Iwdal and Jan Akerblad, this design team was also responsible for the Youth Zone kids and teens center.

For general interiors, Royal Caribbean consulted New York BG Studio of New York. This firm is recognized for its award-winning cruise ship interiors. Partners Francesca Bucci and Hans J. Galutera created the special atmospheres of the Jazz music lounge, the Comedy Live club, and 150 Central Park, the ship's signature fine-dining restaurant.

The unusual and nostalgic hand-carved wooden carousel ride is the work of Ohio's Carousel Works. It is the world's largest manufacturer of hand-carved wooden carousels and succeeds in bringing back the lights, music and magic of the classic carnival carousel.

The ship's retail and shopping venues, including Candy Beach, Star Pier. Pinwheels kids' shop, Prince & Greene, Regalia boutiques and the Focus portrait studio, are all the work of Gensler, the US design and planning firm. This company employs more than 2,100 professionals in 32 offices in Asia, the UK, the Americas and the Middle East.

The Globe and Atlas Pub, Sorrento's Pizzeria, Café Promenade, the

The enormous divide through the center of the ship creates a unique flood of light deep into the heart of Oasis. Photo: © Paul Curtis

Seafood Shack, the Donut Shop, Vintages wine bar and the Park Café are the design work of Elizabeth Sader. Elizabeth is with Morris Nathanson Design on Rhode Island.

Surf machines, volley ball, golf and 82 feet zip line are part of the offerings for active passengers.

A wide choice of pools, some dedicated for adult use only, is available on the upper decks. Photo: © Paul Curtis

The elegant, three-deck Opus main dining room, plus the Casino Royale, the conference center, lobbies, lifts and landings were designed by RTKL from Coral Cables under Greg Walton.

Again, RTKL is no small outfit. It has more than 900 employees and ten offices around the globe. Apart from cruise ships, this company also works on everything from ski resorts and spas to grand hotels in major cities.

The design of the spectacular spa and fitness facility, with its Vitality Café, was the work of a team led by John Picken of Stephenjohn Design in London.

Wilson Butler Architects of Massachusetts provided master planning and led the innovative design work for areas such as the Aqua Theater, Dazzles Nightclub, Entertainment Place, Blaze Nightclub, On Air Club, Opal Theater and the Trellis Bar. They also worked in consort with Atkins Global on the Central Park design.

To this impressive list of consultants, we must not forget to add Royal Caribbean's own in-house team of approximately thirty designers. Established in the late 1990s, the New Building & Fleet Design group (NB&D) works to develop both new-builds and revitalize existing ships. Most importantly, it ensures the all design work is consistent with the company's look and feel throughout the whole Royal Caribbean fleet.

Under the oversight of Design Manager Christopher Love, this team's designs included the Loft Suites, Viking Crown Lounge, Pinnacle Chapel and Lounge, Boleros Latin Bar, the Schooner Bar, the Champagne Bar, Giovanni's Table, Cupcake Cupboard and Pets at Sea.

NB&D design manager Jodi Barozinsky oversaw the external design firms from around the world who contributed to the Oasis.

Working as a cohesive group, these companies took ship design where it had never been before. Before even lifting a single hammer, just completing the design and engineering plans took 1,700,000 hours.

The key outcome of all the meetings and idea exchanges was to break the ship up into distinctly different areas. The design team called these 'neighborhoods' and were especially themed to help passengers immediately feel at home and know where they were.

These districts were named as: Central Park, The Boardwalk, The Royal Promenade, The Pool and Sports Zone, The Vitality Spa and Fitness Center, Entertainment Place and The Youth Zone. Aboard Allure of the Seas, for example, the zones work like this:

Central Park and the Royal Promenade

Deep in the center of the ship, at the base of the cavernous open split pouring light down eight decks, sits Central Park. At 62 feet wide and 328 feet long this area alone is bigger than some cruise ships.

Above the park are the two soaring arched glass domes of the Crystal Canopies. There are also 254 balcony staterooms which with any other design would have just been inside cabins. The view from these balconies must be one of the most extraordinary afloat.

It is a tropical landscape with 12,000 seasonal flowers and shrubs. There are also 27 trees: including Black Olive, Cuban Laurel, Cherry of the Rio Grande, and Painted and Golden Bamboo. Some of the trees are reaching two and half decks in height. Are we really at sea!

Walking the meandering path through the park, visitors come across a chess garden with giant pieces, the Pergola Garden with its vegetation from visited Caribbean islands and a sculpture garden.

Like every good park ashore, there are also quiet corners with seats. This could make for the surreal experience of sitting in a park and reading a book while at sea!

The ship's on-board horticulturist keeps a close eye on the hidden, sophisticated irrigation and drainage and the micro control climate system. For guests seeking to learn more about flora, the horticulturist also gives educational classes

Tranquil and peaceful during the day, at night Central Park's central piazza becomes the ship's town square, a popular gathering space for alfresco dining and street performances.

There are five specialty restaurants in the area covering everything from a signature steakhouse to Tuscan pizza and pasta. There are also upscale boutiques, an art gallery, and a portrait studio. Nearby there is a Starbucks. What more could you want?

Well, there are several bars scattered throughout the Park, including the Canopy Bar located high above in one of the Crystal Canopies. There is also the unique, oval shaped Rising Tide Bar. This rises and descends like a gondola through three decks while transporting 35 people sipping cocktails around an open bar. Truly an engineering feat and while certainly one way of getting high in a bar, it must be the world's oddest elevator.

How on earth did Royal Caribbean come up with that one! Chairman Richard Fain explains:

'There was nothing like it in the original conceptual layouts for the

The full sized carousel has 18 magnificently carved animals each of which took six weeks to make. Photo: © Paul Curtis

The Oasis Carousel is appropriately located on the Boardwalk and it is 23 feet in diameter. Photo: © Paul Curtis

ship. The development of the bar related to the functionality of The Royal Promenade and Central Park.

'These two areas are not only interesting and exciting venues in their own right, they are also an integral part of the fluidity of the ship: they help orient people instinctively to make the ship easier to get around.

'We knew from an early stage that it was important to link these two areas by an easy and dedicated mechanism. The early designs therefore included a couple of small passenger elevators that went between Royal Promenade and Central Park. These two glass elevators were affixed to the side wall going directly between the two levels.

'In looking at the plans, it seemed to me that these elevators were highly functional but very prosaic. They met the need, but they were boring and these spaces deserved better. At that point, I sent an email to Atkins designer Tom Wright with a plea for help.

'Tom responded within an hour with his reaction to my question and a proposed solution. He said he was in Hong Kong, but he agreed that the spaces cried out for something exciting to link them and he attached a WAV file of his initial idea. When I opened the attachment, it was a short video of a man wearing a jet pack and flying off into the atmosphere. I got a good laugh out of that and enjoyed seeing such a terrific imagination at work and at play.

'Somewhat later he came back with a slightly more pragmatic solution. This time, they envisioned an enormous teeter-totter (seesaw) patterned after a child's playground toy. The idea was there would be a small platform at either end of the teeter-totter; when one end was on the Royal Promenade, the other would be at Central Park and vice versa.

'It really was an elegant solution and the mechanism they developed was quite beautiful. It reminded me of one of those fancy Swiss watches where you could see the gears turning and the escapement ratcheting.

'We all liked the idea in concept and marveled at the engineering work they had done to make it feasible. Unfortunately, it required so much space and it carried so few people that we concluded it just wasn't practical.

'It was back to the drawing board and somewhat later, Tom and the Atkins team came back with another terrific idea which became the Rising Tide Bar. Now they proposed a moving bar which could hold a significant number of people and allow those guests to drink while they ride.

'To do this, it had to be certified as an elevator which is no mean feat. As you could imagine, the safety requirements for licensed elevators are quite high, but they had prepared all the engineering and safety systems that made it possible. Our entire team took one look at it and actually applauded at the end of the meeting.'

Concluded Richard Fain, 'We all knew immediately this was a winner. Now that we've seen it in place, we are even more excited about it.'

The Rising Tide Bar concept has gone on to become a feature on all the Oasis class ships.

Pool and Sports Zone

Stretching the long length of the ship, sun worshipers visiting the Pool and Sports Zone discover innovative new twists to conventional ship layout. There are four pools to choose from, including the first beach pool at sea which has a sloped beach type entry. This allow passengers to wade gently into the water rather than having to jump in straight up to the neck.

Being a pool of course, there is no surf. But hang on this is an Oasis ship! So nearby are two forty-feet long flow riders that generate 30 miles per hour waves. These allow surfie types to hang ten all day.

The waves are created by recirculating water at up to 60,000 gallons a minute. There is no fear of either drowning or ever hearing the dreaded drum beat of a Jaws shark attack. Even wipe outs are nice and gentle as the water is only two inches deep and flows over a thick soft rubber base.

If all this sounds too energetic, across from the Beach Pool and separated by Central Park, is the Main Pool with two side-by-side whirlpools. Along with the regular relaxing sun lounger chairs is an area of private cabanas. These have their own dedicated attendant to ensure guests are well looked after.

The younger ones aboard leave older passenger in peace as they head for the wow, fun and excitement of Royal Caribbean's H2O Zone. This is marked by a giant octopus with water-spraying tentacles and slides. All this is surrounded by fellow water-spouting ocean creatures.

There are separate wading and current pools, as well as a dedicated infant and toddler pool. This aquatic playground is circled with both adult and child-sized lounge chairs. You see, these design folks think of everything.

On *Harmony of the Seas*, for thrill seekers, there is a dramatic ten story high water slide. It is called the Ultimate Abyss. And that seems a pretty fair description!

Bigger kids of all ages head for the sports pool to do lap swimming in the

A stroll in Central Park. Photo: © Paul Curtis

morning, or in the afternoon, join in water team events, such as basketball, badminton and water polo.

If this all sounds far too active, another peaceful haven can be found in the adults-only, open-air solarium. This has a swimming pool, two whirlpools, and four cantilevered whirlpools suspended 136 feet above the ocean.

So, while the ship is surrounded by water, there is plenty of it on board as well. Altogether, the ship's swimming pools hold 2,300 tons of water. About the only type pool missing from the mega sisters is a water hazard on the nearby Oasis Dunes nine-hole miniature golf course!

Then of course there is a court for basketball and volleyball. But if you want to get out of the sun for a while, nip a few decks below and go ice skating. The ice rink is huge, so it is just impossible not to go 'wow!' And then just wait until you see the amazing ice shows performed here.

And if that is not enough excitement, adrenalin junkie passengers can go for a ride on the first zip line ever installed on a cruise ship. This is an ideal opportunity to hang from a thin wire nine decks above and then go for an 82 feet long flight through the air. You don't want to miss that one!

Still got more adrenaline to burn? Then go climb one of the two 43 feet high rock walls. These are right at the stern of the ship and offer different climbing tracks for different skill levels. Royal Caribbean says it's free and that they will provide helmets, harnesses and shoes. All you have to do is bring your own socks.

We have only just begun to explore the intent of Royal Caribbean's determination to experience a Mega Sisters' wow factor. So for peace and quiet and less active fun, you can get away from all by taking an amble along the boardwalk.

The Boardwalk

Yes, that's right folks, a boardwalk! Step right up: think Atlantic City, Coney Island, or the pier at Santa Monica. Yes, right here in Oasis City. These ships are absolute architectural miracles.

Of course, no boardwalk is complete without a romantic carousel. And yes, here it is. At 23 feet in diameter, it is not only full-sized, but truly stunning. A 130 square feet of real gold leaf gilding has been used to create a vibrant breath-taking display.

It brings back all the nostalgic memories of childhood and the later sweetheart courting. Eighteen beautifully carved and painted wooden animals

With colorful water fountains playing beneath, the Rising Tide Bar majestically rises through three decks while guests sip their cocktails. This is surely the most unusual elevator in the world. Photo: © Paul Curtis

ride the traditional carousel poles.

It is a complete safari of zebras, giraffes, horses and lions. The meticulous and detailed carving of each animal took six weeks to complete.

Carousel music is the happiest music on earth. Hearing this and seeing the enchantment on people's faces on their colorful whirl makes for a heartwarming experience.

Strolling on down the boardwalk we pass an art gallery and six shops. There's also five restaurants and bars including a The Shack Seafood Restaurant. Nearby is a wonderful Johnny Rockets recreation of a 1940's diner. You can just march in anytime for malts, shakes, French fries or a hamburger.

At the aft end of the boardwalk we come to the Aqua Theater. This is a 750-seat outdoor arena modeled on an ancient Greek amphitheater. Again, it is another amazing example of the Oasis quest for the wow factor. It is the largest and deepest saltwater pool at sea. It is 21.9 feet by 51.6 feet wide and has a depth of 17.9 feet.

Why so deep? Well the pool has a diving tower with two spring boards and two 33-feet high-dive platforms. These, you will be relieved to know, are not for the use of passengers! Although the kidney-shaped pool is overlooked by sun loungers on tiered platforms during the day and offers swimming and scuba diving, its main purpose is to host the most stunning entertainment ever seen at sea.

Royal Caribbean scoured the world for eighteen Olympic and National Collegiate Athletic Association champions. Most shows include six divers, plus a further two specialty divers, four synchronized swimmers, and six gymnasts. Together they perform acrobatics, synchronized swimming, water ballet and the high-diving.

The Aqua Theater set-up itself is jaw dropping. It would be hard to find its equal in a huge sporting complex ashore let alone on a ship at sea. There are three underwater stage lifts which can be raised to various levels from below water during a performance. There are three underwater cameras to film performers under water.

The images are projected onto two giant Barco LED screens set each side of the main stage area. A giant trampoline is centered between the two diving towers. A high bridge connecting the two dive towers can support an entire row of divers. A trapeze hangs behind the high dive boards. On the underbelly of this bridge are lights and nozzles to create a colorful waterfall onto the pool below.

Under the magic of a night time sky, below two overhead audio-visual control booths which handle projection, lighting, special effects, sound and cameras, an all-star cast performs a heart-pounding, dramatic spectacular. It always brings the audience to its feet.

The Aqua Theater never rests. Throughout the evenings, programmed to music and lights, hundreds of water nozzles, some able to shoot 65 feet high, perform beautiful choreographed fountain shows. One of the water jet nozzles is nicknamed 'gargoyle' and shoots high enough to hit the Crown & Anchor RCI logo over the pool.

Entertainment place

In addition to the Aqua Theater and the main theater, at Entertainment Place there is an intimate live jazz and blues lounge; a live comedy theater, the huge ice rink with its stellar cast of ice skaters and a two-floor dance lounge.

The main indoor theater seats 1,380 in armchair comfort. The technical lighting and sound is the envy of many a Broadway theater. Twelve technical staff work the complex staging. This even allows a fashion catwalk platform to magically slide out deep into the midst of the audience.

The stage show productions and talent are world class. For instance, Allure of the Seas launched with an exclusive entertainment program developed by DreamWorks Animation. Indeed, Princess Fiona of the famous 'Shrek' movie accepted the honor of being this ship's inaugural godmother.

On the introduction of the Oasis of the Seas, The Tony award-winning Broadway musical, 'Hairspray,' was licensed to Royal Caribbean International for three years. Then followed a production of the ever-popular Andrew Lloyd Webber show 'Cats.' And if stage shows aren't your thing, then of course, you can always go the movies...in 3D of course.

While on the entertainment front, remember a cruise on one of the mega sisters of the seas will also save you a trip to Las Vegas. Naturally enough, these ships feature the largest and most sophisticated casinos afloat. There are themed walkway entrances and special displays such as a museum of gaming to explore the history of gambling.

Design elements include dramatic sculptures and a crystal chandelier with hues of amethyst, aquamarine and ruby. It's a really classy place to lose your money! Amidst the glitter, you will find 450 slot machines, tables for blackjack, roulette, craps, and Caribbean stud poker, a bar, a lounge area, a sports book, a poker room and a players' club. And aboard a ship of this size,

The Aqua Theater Pool hosts a stunning visual display of acrobatics, high diving in a pool with three different rising stages from below the water. Photo: © Paul Curtis

Photo: © Paul Curtis

The roomy scene poolside reflects in the floor to ceiling observation windows above. Photo: © Paul Curtis

The huge Aqua pool theater with its giant screens and the two rock climbing walls. Photo: © Paul Curtis

Photo: © Paul Curtis

Surfing the two Flow Riders. Photo: © Paul Curtis

Flying high on the 82 feet zip line. Photo: © Paul Curtis

the only roll you will ever experience is the roll of the dice.

If you are after a little more culture, Oasis ships have that too. Royal Caribbean has acquired one of the world's largest private art collections for display on its fleet of ships.

At last count, it was valued at $120 million and includes pop-culture icons such as Romero Britto and Thomas Kinkade, limited-edition signed photography, prints and objects, and one-off pieces, reliefs and miniatures. Aboard an Oasis ship there are around 7000 art pieces on display. Special art tours, seminars and auctions are organized for art enthusiasts.

Vitality at Sea Spa and Fitness Centre

Back in 1970, Song of Norway, Royal Caribbean's first ship, had a gym in an empty cabin that consisted of a rowing machine and a treadmill. Not many people used the gym or made any effort to find it. Things have come a long way since then. Today, Royal Caribbean's newest ships feature the largest fitness centers and spas at sea. They swarm with passenger activity.

Pools that were once inside the ship and on the lowest level have evolved into entire water-parks and pool-scapes running the length of the uppermost decks.

So, for those fearful of having piled on too many calories in one of the 24 restaurants, then it's time to head for the Spa and Fitness Zone. The Vitality at Sea Spa includes a thermal suite with heated tile loungers, saunas and steam rooms. There are three massage suites for couples and seven individual treatment rooms. Young children and teen passengers have their own dedicated spa. This makes it the largest spa at sea.

The Fitness Center offers a large and varied range of cardio and resistance equipment. There are also work out classes for spinning, kick-boxing, pilates and yoga. On Deck three, there is the longest-running track on any passenger ship. It is 0.43 miles in length and if you stagger round just a couple of times you have just about done your first mile. It is also partly covered so you neither get sunburnt or windblown. When you work out works up a hunger, you can stop by The Vitality Café for healthy snacks, light meals and refreshing juices.

The Youth Zone

The Youth Zone neighborhood spans more than 28,700 square feet, and it is again, of course, the largest at sea. On Kids Avenue, there are themed play areas: a nursery for infants and toddlers and a teenager heaven. On offer are

Looking up through all the decks makes for an appreciation of the sheer grandeur and size of these vessels. Photo: © Paul Curtis

arts and crafts activities, scavenger hunts and show business help for those entering the passenger talent shows

In addition to the dedicated spaces for each of the three age groups, Oasis ships features several common play areas. These include the first-ever theater at sea just for kids. This comes complete with a stage and curtains, audience seating and state-of-the-art production equipment. The ships also run special youth workshops which include creating scrapbooks, designing jewelry and drama.

For the budding scientist, there is the Adventure Science Lab. This is well-equipped and although not quite up to splitting the atom, it is perfect for conducting baking soda volcanoes.

'Play' is a circular area where the kids can participate in a variety of sports covering everything from basketball to soccer. There is also a dedicated arcade space just for the under twelves.

For the teens, there is The Living Room, which boasts a 'mocktail' bar offering alcohol-free concoctions, and scratch DJ 101 classes. Here youngsters can learn how to spin their own beats. There is a bank of computers for web surfing. Nearby is a disco called Fuel. This serves as a hangout space with a dance floor and gives outdoor deck space.

In the Vitality Spa, children and teen passengers have their own dedicated spa. With all these facilities and activities, taking the family on a cruise should prove fun for the youngsters and relaxing for the parents.

So that's the seven separate Oasis zones. Whereas it would be unfair to call them the Seven Deadly Sins, they certainly cannot deny being seven areas of extreme indulgence!

All Access Tour

A good way to explore the rest of the ships it to take the all access tour. There is a charge for this as it can only be done in very small groups. The charge makes sure that all those ship enthusiasts that really want to know the back of house scenes will get the opportunity.

The tour takes you below decks, backstage of the main theater, engine control room, into the galleys and up onto the bridge. You also get to meet the officers and crew who can explain all the various operations they control.

Under the watchful and caring eye of a crew member, you also get to walk along the I-95 Highway. It is very aptly named after the USA's busiest highway, although many claim that as crew come from so many different nationalities it is named after the USA Immigration form. With separate lanes for motorized vehicles and pedestrians, this hidden service corridor bustles with traffic and runs the entire length of the ship.

It's a long trip and indeed, one of the Oasis captains invoked his master's

On Oasis, two officers are always on watch duty The view of the bridge from the heliport.
Captain Johnny's scooter getting a quick recharge in a corner of the bridge. Photos: © Paul Curtis

privilege and keeps a motor scooter on the bridge. He uses it to make his inspections fast and efficiently. This is Captain Johnny Faevelen. He has both a Harley motorcycle and a scooter. He also has a parrot. So, if you are on an Oasis ship and see the captain on a motor cycle with a parrot on his shoulder, you will know that you have found Captain Johnny. Even the Oasis captain can have the wow factor!

The scooter could also come in handy on the bridge as this area is enormous. It is 215 feet from one side of the bridge to the other. The wings, or ends, of the bridge project over the ship's sides so that during docking maneuvers the captain has perfect visibility of the ship's position in relation to the wharf.

The captain makes a weekly inspection of every aspect of the ship. On other days, he is out and about talking to passengers. He will proudly explain how the ship's smoke stacks are retractable to allow the ship to pass under the Belt Way Bridge in Denmark. There is no use for this feature elsewhere on the world itinerary, but the functions are still regularly tested.

He will also tell you that the Allure's $1.3 billion cost was before the filling of the gas tanks! The ship uses 600,000 gallons every day and carries plenty of reserve fuel. In fact, the ship carries enough fuel to take the ship from Miami to Europe and then back again.

On a normal cruise schedule, refueling takes place every fourteen days. Barges loaded with fuel are brought alongside to complete the bunkering process.

The same vein of keeping plenty of reserves is also applied to human fuel. A ship can overrun its normal cruise schedule by at least two days before any thought need to be given to re-supply or breaking into emergency rations.

Captain Johnny is extremely proud of his ship's stability. Due to its wide beam, it gives an extremely smooth ride, even in rough seas. As soon as the ship tilts a mere half of one degree, the stabilizers are deployed.

This is in stark contrast to some ships, which in order to save fuel costs, only deploy their stabilizers when the ship has already started to roll. And once such a ship really begins to roll, putting out the stabilizers a little too late has a lessened and delayed effect.

Safety is paramount aboard Oasis ships. Each one carries eighteen very large lifeboats. In their own right, these are very seaworthy and can hold 370 people in each. Most ships' lifeboats have a capacity limited to eighty people.

The advantage of this design approach is that as less ship space is crowded with individual lifeboats more cabins can enjoy uncluttered sea views. In addition to the lifeboats, the ship also carries many additional safety floats.

For such a huge ship, the Oasis class is surprisingly maneuverable. Once Captain Johnny demonstrated this to another ship of the line by passing her at sea while going backwards! This caused passenger amazement on both ships.

The Cabins

With the introduction of the split interior and the park beneath, Royal Caribbean took the opportunity to tear up traditional cabin layouts. It came up with a design that allowed cabins to have interior views of the park and the boardwalk. This gives both natural light and an interesting view.

Another industry-first is the introduction of twenty-eight contemporary two-level loft suites. Each loft measures 545 square feet. If you have so many friends this is still not big enough, you can also connect to an adjoining suite.

The lofts are the highest tiered accommodations at sea and with floor-to-ceiling, double-height windows give spectacular views of the ocean. The view inside is equally impressive, especially from the upper-level bedroom that overlooks both the living area and the sea.

This is spacious living at its best and the lofts are decorated with abstract, modern art pieces. And of course, there is a private balcony with sun chairs

The lofts feature extra-large LCD televisions, separate vanity areas, a guest bathroom downstairs and an upstairs master bathroom with an en suite featuring his and hers shower heads and fog-free mirrors. Now that's class!

The Royal Loft Suite is the largest of the lofts. These are fitted out with everything from a baby grand piano, indoor and outdoor dining rooms, a private wet bar, a library and an extended balcony with its own LCD television set. Add to this, an entertainment area and a jacuzzi and you are all set up! In total, it measures 148.5 square meters, plus the balcony of course!

Still not big enough? The Royal Loft Suite can connect to a Crown Loft Suite for additional room to accommodate a total of ten guests.

All in all, there are 2700 staterooms and at double occupancy the Oasis ships can sleep from between 5,400 to more than 6000 guests.

Balcony suites have a good-sized private balcony to sit and watch the world go by. There are also eight Boardwalk view window staterooms.

Those opting for the economical inside staterooms, even though they are minus a porthole, the view outside can still be monitored on the TV via the ship's bridge camera. So, all is not lost and apart from saving some money, these are particularly suited to those who party all night.

The bedding: the mattresses, pillows, sheets and duvets, are all made, especially for Royal Caribbean in Italy. Rest assured. You will be comfortable.

In fact, many guests are so taken with it all that they order the ship's bedding on-line to be delivered to their own homes.

To stuff them all into your own suitcases is not an option. This collection is far too fluffy and voluminous for that!

Top: ocean view stateroom; Middle: loft suite; Lower: royal loft suite.

Relaxation room in the Vitality Spa. Photo: © Paul Curtis

Oasis of the Seas and Allure of the Seas meeting for the first time off Fort Lauderdale.

The first step in ship building is the laying of the keel. Here we see the first section of Harmony being laid into position.

The first Oasis ship under construction.

Allure approaching completion.

Chapter Three

Building the Dream

Building any type of ship is a huge project, but to build not only the biggest ship in the world, but five of them, one after the other, is a feat beyond compare.

All five ships have been built by STX Europe. With headquarters in Oslo, Norway, in 2015 the company had fifteen shipyards operating in Brazil, Finland, France, Norway, Romania and Vietnam.

The evolution of STX Europe originated with the founding of two prominent shipbuilding groups. One was the Norway based Aker Yards, created in 2004 by combining the shipbuilding activities of Aker and Kværner with the France-based Alstom shipbuilding group. Alstom also owned the Chantiers de l'Atlantique shipyard in Saint-Nazaire. This was the yard that built the Queen Mary 2, which at the time of its launch was the biggest passenger ship in the world. But she is only a sprat when compared to the Oasis class ships.

The first two ships, Oasis and Allure, were built in STX's Turku shipyard in Finland while Harmony and Symphony and the new fifth ship, all come from STX in France. The fifth Oasis ship will be delivered in Spring of 2021

The design project began in 2003 and the first vessel, Oasis of the Seas, was officially ordered in February 2006. The key step is to lay down the keel and this was first done in STX Europe's Finland shipyard on the 12 November 2007. After the keel laying, the build was completed in two years. To build a ship of this size in that time was a stunning achievement. The completed ship was handed over to Royal Caribbean on October 28, 2009 and she entered service two months later.

The significant step of keel laying is marked with a special ceremony in the builders' yard and it is attended by all the key participants. With champagne, and speeches the department heads gather together to witness and celebrate the first building step. For an Oasis ship this is not one small step for mankind. A giant crane lifts into the building dock and carefully and precisely lays a pre-cut 1,000-ton block of steel measuring 32 feet by 154 feet

The stern of Oasis begins to take shape.

A building block moving into position for Harmony.

Royal Caribbean's Chairman and CEO Richard D. Fain taking a keen interest in the first Oasis ship construction.

The steel cutting ceremony for Oasis 4 at the STX shipyard in Saint-Nazaire. Left to right: Jean-Yves Jaouen, SVP, Operations, STX France; Jean-Yves Pean, Senior Project Manager, STX France; Pettri Keso, Project Manager, Royal Caribbean International; Harri Kulovaara, Executive Vice President, Newbuild, Royal Caribbean Cruises Ltd, and Laurent Castaing, chief executive officer, STX France.

Turning the valve to float the first Oasis are Richard Fain, Harri Kulovaara, Martin Landtman and Toivo Ilvonen.

and gently lowers it into place.

In accordance with maritime tradition, newly minted coins are positioned under the keel. These stay in place until the end of the ship's construction. The coins are then retrieved and presented to the ship's captain and crew to be displayed on-board the ship.

Sailors are a superstitious lot and believe the coins will bring luck to the ship during its construction process and forevermore to the captains and crew that sail on her. The coins, however, are the least expensive part of the investment. The total build cost for the first Oasis ship was estimated at $1.24 billion dollars!

Of course, laying the keel, which is really the backbone of the ship, is just the beginning and for an Oasis class there are another 180 blocks to go. Block construction is a modern shipbuilding method which involves the assembly of prefabricated multi-deck cross-sections of the superstructure. These can be 230 to 260 feet high and include pre-installed pipes, plumbing and electrical cables.

Once completed, they are taken to the building dock and then hoisted or even floated into position and then welded into place. Putting together all the building blocks of an Oasis-class ship makes it the world's biggest jigsaw puzzle.

Each of the pre-assembled blocks of the ship weigh in the region of 1,322,772 pounds, or if you prefer, 600 metric tons.

Altogether, there are 500,000 individual steel parts and for the first Oasis it took more than 8000 work years to build her. Fortunately, to speed things up a bit, there were more than 3,200 construction workers at any given time!

They had to lay 150 miles of pipework, 3,300 miles of electrical cabling and rig 100,000 lighting points and fit out 2706 cabins.

Once it is all put together, the final finishing paint touches are added. Painting the ship inside and out, takes 158,503 gallons (600,000 liters) of paint. That's nearly sixteen times more paint slapping than it takes to cover from one end to the other of San Francisco's Golden Gate Bridge.

Behind the bulbous bow can be seen the four holes for the bow thrusters.

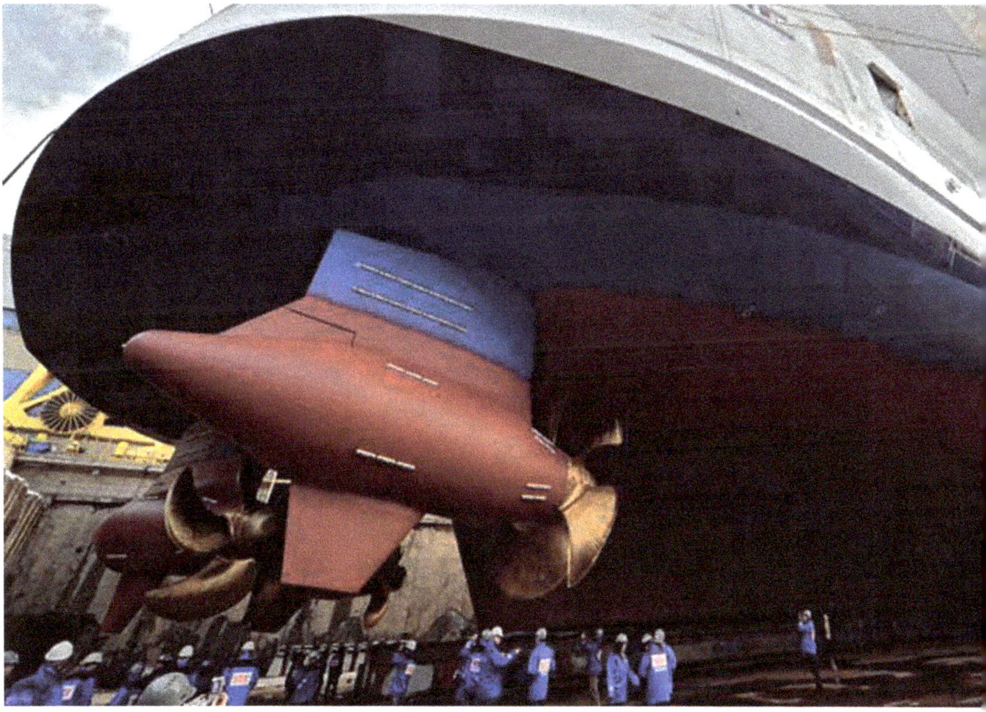

At the stern hangs three enormous Azimuth pods that can be rotated to steer the ship in any direction.

June 2015: The newest member of the Oasis class, Harmony of the Seas,- floated out of her dry dock to begin the next phase of interior construction.

Chapter Four

Powering the Behemoths

Well, we now have our 225,282-gross registered tonnes of ship, 1,187 feet long, 208 feet wide, and approximately 20 stories high. As you can imagine, the electrical power requirements are enormous.

The whole ship is air-conditioned and there are 16 passenger decks, 24 passenger elevators, 6,296 guests and the 2165 crew members from more than sixty-five countries. And every one of them wants hot meals. Then there's twenty-three tonnes of water in the twenty-one swimming pools and jacuzzis that needs to be heated. Now add the power demands of refrigeration for all the food storage and don't forget the need to produce fifty tons of ice cubes each day. To flick the light switch, for this little lot, just imagine how fast the electricity meter spins!

However, that's not the biggest demand for power. The ship needs to move as well! Indeed, these floating Oasis class self-contained cities clip along under electric motors at an average cruising speed of more than 26 miles an hour. In more nautical terms that's 22.6 knots.

The ship's engines are essentially just a power plant that produces electricity, which is then used to run everything on board. The majority is used for propelling the vessel. Air conditioning comes second in power demand.

One of the most famous manufacturers of marine engines for cruise ships is the Finnish corporation Wärtsilä. Their engines are equipped with common rail technology, which provides an important and an almost invisible advantage. As the combustion and other process parameters can be adjusted for lower load ranges, smoke emissions can be reduced.

With its main focus on improving efficiency and minimizing emissions, Wärtsilä continuously aims to improve the environmental performance of its engines. For Oasis of the Seas a total of six Wärtsilä 46 engines, three 12-cylinder and three 16-cylinder engines, generating more than 96 MW were installed. Each of these engines is the size of a school bus!

The vessel was also equipped with four 5.5 MW (7,500 horse power) Wärtsilä bow thrusters. Fittingly, these are among the largest in the world.

The bow thrusters are used to push the bow of a vessel to either side during docking procedures. This enables this huge ship to be safely docked without the use of tug boats.

The Wärtsilä bow thrusters have a combined power output of 22 MW. In fact, the bow thrusters alone have more power than is installed on a normal cargo ship. The fuel consumption of the main engines at full power is 1,377 US gallons per engine per hour for the 16-cylinder engines and 1,033 US gallons per engine per hour for the 12-cylinder engines. The total output of these prime movers is 97,020 kilowatts (130,110 horse power) and this is converted to electricity.

Instead of the conventional engine shafted propellers and rudders, propulsion and steering is done by three huge propellers suspended under the stern which can rotate in any direction. The electric motors that drive these 20-feet diameter propellers are underneath the hull in a pod like structure not too dissimilar from that of a very huge outboard motor.

Called Azipods, each of the three pods has an electric motor that can run at 20,000-kilowatt (26,800 horse power) The Azipods are made by ABB, another leading Finnish company. Because they are rotatable in any direction, no rudders are needed to steer the ship.

In addition to superior maneuverability, ABB's Azipods also deliver fuel efficiency, with savings of around ten to fifteen per cent compared to conventional shaft-line propulsion systems. This reduces fuel costs and cuts greenhouse gas emissions.

The units are also far quieter and more compact than alternatives, allowing ship designers to utilize the machinery spaces more efficiently. As they are so powerful, they can drive the huge Oasis ships as fast as 24 knots but offer a comfortable cruising speed of 22 knots. That works out at approximately 26 miles per hour or 42 kilometers per hour.

Royal Caribbean's strict environmental policies lead to the ships being fitted with solar panels to provide energy for lighting in the Promenade and Central Park areas. The installation on deck nineteen cost US$750,000 and covers 1,950 square meters (21,000 square feet). Each ship's desalination plant produces 4,700,000 lbs. (2,350 metric tons) of fresh water for consumption every 24 hours and it is stored in 31 huge tanks.

No sewage is discharged into the sea and all water is treated and reused on board. Don't forget there are those twelve thousand plus plants to water!

The Oasis of the Seas and the Allure of the Seas were the most energy efficient cruise ships in the world. But the design team is always striving

Celebrating the delivery of the Oasis of the Seas are Adam Goldstein, President and CEO, Royal Caribbean International, Richard Fain, Chairman and CEO of Royal Caribbean Cruises and Harri Kulovaara, EVP, New build and Design.

From an air-conditioned control room, engineers monitor all the ship's functions. Photo: © Paul Curtis

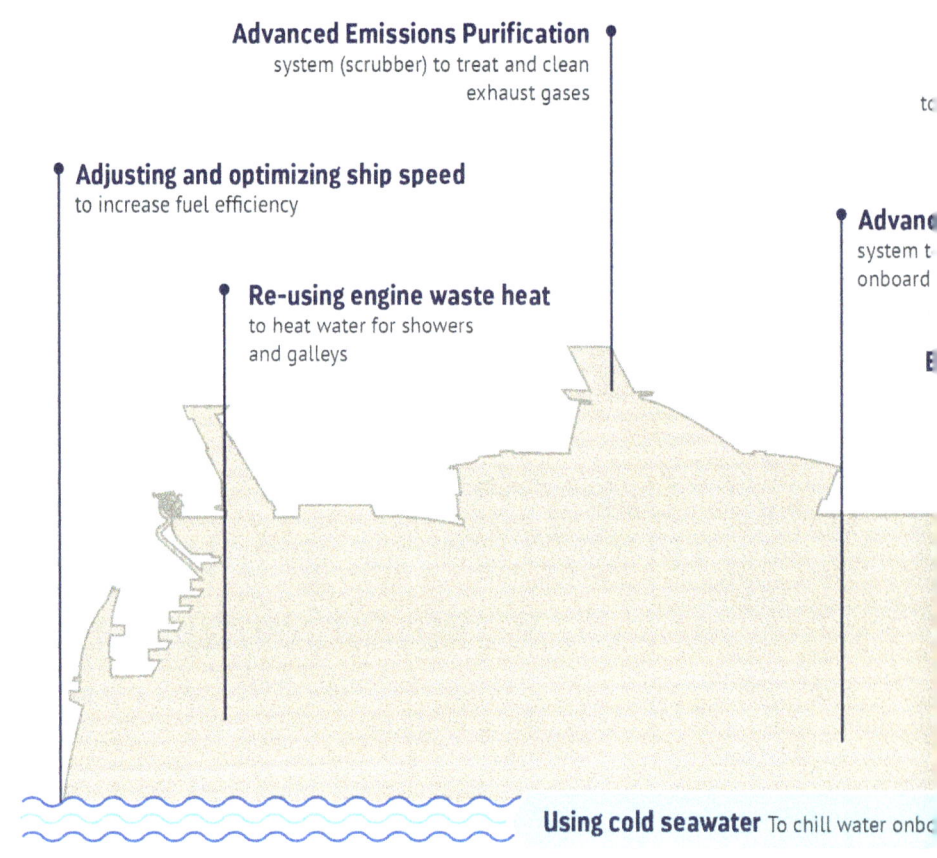

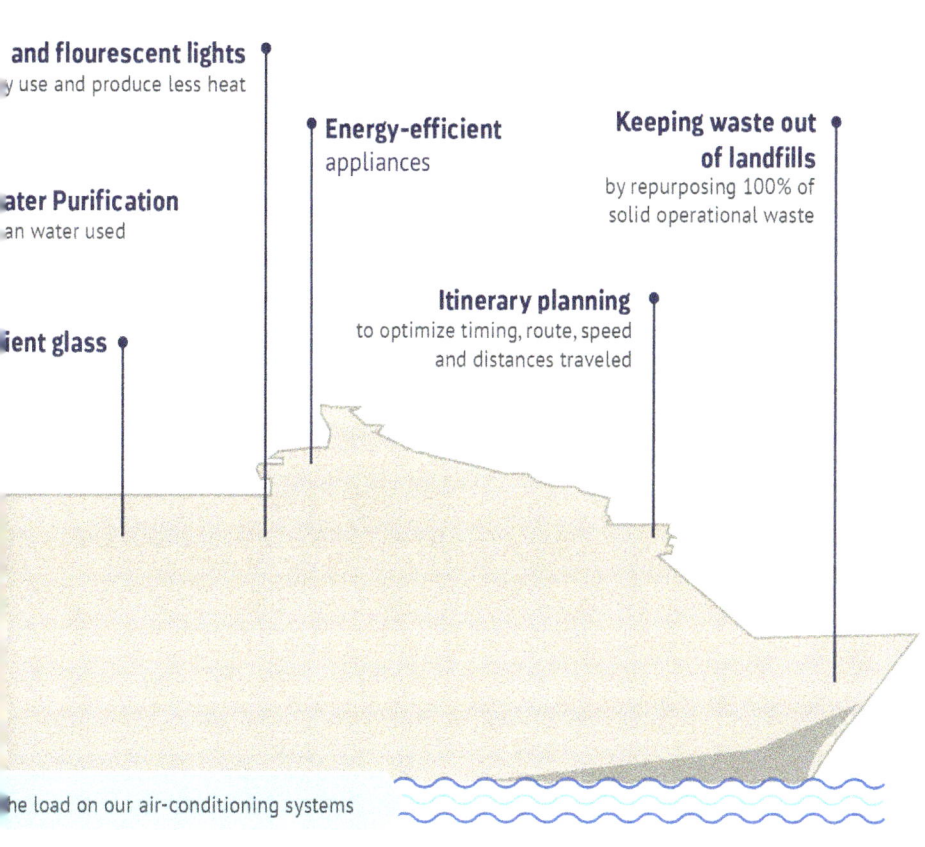

and flourescent lights
y use and produce less heat

Energy-efficient appliances

Keeping waste out of landfills
by repurposing 100% of solid operational waste

ater Purification
an water used

Itinerary planning
to optimize timing, route, speed and distances traveled

ient glass

he load on our air-conditioning systems

system
ative species

Air lubrication system
to reduce drag and increase fuel efficiency

for continual improvement and Harmony is approximately twenty percent more energy efficient than her first two sisters. This has been achieved by adopting LED lighting and installing two air compressors which release a stream of billions of microscopic bubbles under the hull of a ship. Known as air lubrication, it reduces water friction and improves fuel efficiency as the ship glides along on the bubbles.

A different and more efficient engine configuration consists of four 12-cylinder Wärtsilä 46F engines and two 16-cylinder Wärtsilä 46F engines. The heat from these engines is utilized to power a steam engine generator. Two Wärtsilä scrubbers have been installed to clean exhaust gases before they leave the ship. Ninety percent of sulfur dioxide is removed along with a significant reduction of nitrogen oxides and particulates.

The steam generated by the engines is also used to power a turbine to generate more electricity. The ship's engine room now hosts 150 crew to keep everything is smooth working order.

The quest for increased environmental efficiency is never ending. Royal Caribbean and the Meyer Turku shipyard have announced their joint intention to develop the next generation of LNG powered cruise ships including the application of fuel cells for power generation.

When, in 2022, shipbuilder Meyer Turku deliver the first Icon class ship for Royal Caribbean, she will be primarily powered by liquefied natural gas (LNG) and the use of fuel cell technology. Recognizing that at this early stage there are several ports that cannot yet offer LNG bunkering, the ship will also be able to run on distillate fuel. However, in pursuit of a cleaner environment and taking the smoke out of the smokestacks, RCI's support will undoubtedly propel more ports into building suitable facilities.

Royal Caribbean is testing fuel cell technology on an Oasis class ship and is running progressively larger fuel cell projects on new vessels being built. Fuel cells are a very energy efficient and a clean way to generate electrical energy. Although still at an early stage, as the technology becomes smaller and more efficient, fuel cells become more viable and significant in their ability to power a cruise ship's hotel functions. The advantage of this is reduced air emission and noise, improved fuel efficiency and the ability to meet increasingly stringent environmental regulations.

The use of the fuel cell as an electricity generator was invented by William Grove and dates to as long ago as 1842. It consists of a mix of fuel and gas converting electrochemical reactions to electric power. It works in a similar manner to a battery where electrochemical reactions occur between the

CRUISE SHIP  OF THE FUTURE

LIQUEFIED NATURAL GAS IS CONSIDERED TO BE THE **CLEANEST-BURNING** FOSSIL FUEL

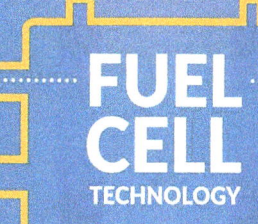

FUEL CELL TECHNOLOGY CAN HELP **REDUCE SHIP EMISSIONS**

Fuel cells generate electricity by chemical reaction with very **LITTLE POLLUTION**

RCL'S AIR LUBRICATION SYSTEM IS A CURTAIN OF MICROSCOPIC BUBBLES THAT COATS THE SHIP HULL AND **REDUCES DRAG**

LNG is produced by taking natural gas from a production field, removing impurities, and liquefying the natural gas

LNG PRODUCES NO SULFUR AND HAS **LOWER NITROUS OXIDE EMISSIONS** AND **LESS SOOT**

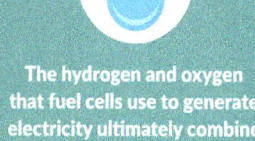

The hydrogen and oxygen that fuel cells use to generate electricity ultimately combine to form water

THE WATER CAN BE INGESTED, PUT TO OTHER USES OR BE DISCARDED AS WASTE

NASA has been using fuel cells for decades

THE POWER FUEL CELLS PRODUCED **SUPPLIED ELECTRICITY ON SPACECRAFT** AND CREW MEMBERS DRANK THE WATER

FUEL CELLS DO NOT BURN ANYTHING TO PRODUCE POWER, SO THERE ARE **NO EMISSIONS TO HARM THE ENVIRONMENT**

anode or cathode and the electrolyte membrane. The difference with a fuel cell is that it is fed with a continuous fuel and air supply.

This was appealing for use in such specialist areas as spaceships and submarines, but for general use such as in motor cars, the efficiency of combustion engines led to simpler and more economical paths being adopted. However, with today's rising oil costs, coupled with the demand to lower pollution levels, improving fuel cells, has been declared as the way to the technology of the future. This will have a huge impact on the shipping industry.

RCI says today's technology and regulations are not yet ready for extensive maritime use, but the pilot installations it is making are the stepping stones to a new era of shipbuilding and will dramatically reduce greenhouse gas emissions.

Sea trials inside Harmony's engine room.

Sea trials aboard Harmony.

Chapter Five

The Maiden Voyage

Naming a ship is a very important step for a cruise company. And when you first announce the build of not one but the two biggest passenger ships in the world, it takes on even greater significance.

Whereas in the past, Royal Caribbean had deferred to the wishes of various directors, for this project they took the unprecedented step of giving the naming opportunity to the general public.

In January 2008, in partnership with the newspaper USA Today, the public were invited to submit two names that best encapsulated the Royal Caribbean cruise experience. All the contest stipulated was that the names had to end in the words 'of the Seas'.

There were more than 91,000 entries in this 'Name That Ship', contest. Four months later, the winning combination of names was announced: *Oasis of the Seas and Allure of the Seas*. These were submitted by George Weiser, of Livonia, Michigan. Weiser's contribution also earned him the honor of naming the entire class of the new ships and the title Project Genesis was dropped in favor of referring to the new ships as the Oasis class.

In February 2015, Royal Caribbean announced that the third Oasis class ship would be named Harmony of the Seas and that steel cutting had begun on a fourth Oasis ship that was to be named later as Symphony of the Seas.

Although the names have been chosen before 'float out' from the shipyard, the official naming ceremony only takes place after the final delivery of the vessel. After the official keel laying ceremony, the next major celebration is the float out.

For the launch of the first Oasis, Royal Caribbean Cruises executives: Richard Fain, chairman and CEO and Harri Kulovaara, executive vice president, flew into Finland to join Martin Landtman, president, STX Finland and Toivo Ilvonen, the project director.

On November 21, 2008, these four put their hands together on the huge valve that floods the construction dock and thus floats the ship for the very first time into her natural environment.

Photos: © Paul Curtis

Said an enthused Richard Fain, 'We've waited a long time to see this all together. She has now come to life. This is a historic day for our company. After more than three years of intense planning and collaboration and with 65 percent of the ship already complete, it's exciting to see Oasis entering its final stages'

The line chose the occasion to announce that Oasis of the Seas would enter service under the command of Captain William S. Wright and Captain Tor Olsen. Wright, a fifteen-year veteran of Royal Caribbean International, was also the start-up Captain for Freedom of the Seas, previously the largest ship in the world. But Freedom, together with her sister-ships Liberty and Independence, were forty percent smaller than Oasis.

Wright was one of the few American captains in international cruising and was also serving as the senior vice president of Marine Operations for the cruise line.

Captain Tor Olsen was born in Norway and like many from this great seafaring nation, went to sea at the age of sixteen. He joined Royal Caribbean International in 1987 and served as Captain on five Royal Caribbean ships from the Voyager class to the Vision class.

After the floating out ceremony, it took a further eleven months to apply the finishing touches before she was finally handed over to her new owners on October 28th, 2009 in Turku. To mark this milestone the ship's flag of Finland is ceremoniously lowered and replaced with the Royal Caribbean house flag.

The Voyage Home

Two days later, Oasis of the Seas left Turku for her new home port of Fort Lauderdale in America. Her first challenge on leaving the Baltic Sea was a midnight pass underneath the Great Belt Bridge. This connects the Danish islands of Zealand and Funen.

Although late at night, hundreds of people gathered on beaches on both sides to witness the event. For safety reasons, traffic at each end of the bridge was stopped.

This was because the bridge has a clearance height of 65 meters and the Oasis of Seas is 72 meters tall. This fact was of course well anticipated, and the designers had devised unusual retracting telescopic funnels. The ship was also able to reduce its height by flooding its forward and aft balance tanks with 4,000 tons of water made by the ship's own fresh water makers.

Captain William Wright in command of the first Atlantic crossing for Oasis of the Seas.

Allure squeezing under the Great Belt Bridge in daytime rather than the midnight passage made under here by Oasis of the Seas.

Then the ship's officers factored into their calculations the 'squat effect'. This results in the fact that a vessel traveling at speed in a shallow channel will be drawn deeper into the water. This was calculated to sink the ship by a further twelve inches (30 centimeters).

So, with all calculations done, imagine the heart-in-mouth moment of charging the bridge with a brand-new ship at 23 miles per hour to pass under with a clearance of only a few inches! But that's what they did. They ended up with less than two feet. Fortunately, in this very exacting science, everyone had got their sums right!

Moving on through to the English Channel, the Oasis stopped briefly off Southampton in the Solent to disembark 300 shipyard workers who were still on-board doing finishing touches.

Southampton's many shipping enthusiasts thronged every vantage point to catch a glimpse of the ship three times the size of the QE2 and five times bigger than the Titanic. The skies were filled with helicopters as the media vied for the best sneak preview footage of the unannounced but spectacular arrival.

With Captain William S. Wright in command, the ship then began her journey across the winter Atlantic to Fort Lauderdale. As many a former ship's passenger can attest, a winter crossing of the Atlantic often proves less than the smoothest passage.

During the design process, comprehensive laboratory model testing had been done at every stage. These included wind, sea and catastrophic damage simulations. The design had come through with flying colors. However, this was the real thing.

The seas built to more than forty feet and the winds neared hurricane force. The designers had created a very wide hull but only 31 feet sits beneath the water. Such designs can cause a ship to snap back upright sharply after a wave has passed, but with the Oasis of the Seas, her huge size minimizes the impact of large waves.

The ship's officers were delighted with her performance under these testing sea conditions.

Oasis arrived at Fort Lauderdale on 13 November 2009, fourteen days after leaving Finland's port of Turku. She was right on schedule and hundreds of people turned out to get their first glimpse of the world's most revolutionary ship.

During the next six days, the ship began her final preparations for her first passenger carrying cruise. There were all the tropical gardens to plant and the

The huge ship towers above passengers returning from an island excursion tour.

A Zip line rider flies down from high above the stern.
Photos: © Paul Curtis

complex staging for the various theater performances to be installed.

The first performer to take the stage on Oasis of the Seas was the pop music artist Rihanna, On November 19, Oasis made her national television premiere when she hosted ABC's Good Morning America program.

Next came the official naming ceremony on Monday, November 30. This was a gala event in aid of the Make-A-Wish Foundation. In a break with the tradition of naming one godmother for the vessel, Royal Caribbean thought for a ship of this size they should not have just one, but seven godmothers! The idea is that each godmother would represent one of the special, seven neighborhoods created.

Each of the godmothers was chosen because they personify strength of character, exemplify the spirit of giving, and are role models for men, women and children alike. They were all known for their extensive and long commitment to charity work.

The selected godmothers were: Gloria Estefan, world-renowned singer, songwriter, actor and author; Michelle Kwan, Olympic Games medalist and the most decorated figure skater in United States history; Jane Seymour, the award winning actor; Dara Torres, the swimming champion who is a twelve-time Olympic medalist; Keshia Knight Pulliam, film and television actress; Shawn Johnson, women's gymnastics Olympic Games medalist for women's gymnastics and cancer philanthropist and Daisy Fuentes, international television personality and producer, beauty and fitness expert.

After the gala night, the ship was off the very next morning on a four-night pre-inaugural sailing to Royal Caribbean's own private beach destination of Labadee in Haiti. This was immediately followed on December 5, 2009 by the ship's official inaugural cruise calling at the popular destinations of St. Thomas, St. Maarten and Nassau.

It is easy to imagine that with all this going on the shipping company well and truly had its hands full. But coming hot on the heels of Oasis of the Seas was the second ship: Allure of the Seas.

Ordered on the April 2, 2007, Allure's keel was laid on December 2, 2008 in the same STX Turku shipyard that had seen Oasis floated out just twelve days before. Allure was floated out from dry dock to wet dock on November 23, 2009. This float out also ended Oasis claim to be the biggest passenger ship in the world as Allure measured just two inches longer!

At the float ceremony for Allure, President and CEO of Royal Caribbean International, Adam Goldstein commented, 'Oasis of the Seas has been welcoming her first guests these past few days, and to think that Allure of the

Seas will follow suit in just one short year is just extraordinary.'

Allure was officially handed over to the company on October 28, 2010 and with Captain Hernan Zini at the helm, Allure of the Seas left Turku the next day to begin her thirteen-day passage to Fort Lauderdale.

On her maiden arrival on November 11, 2010, the shores of Fort Lauderdale were just as crowded and enthusiastic as those that greeted Oasis just a year before. Thousands of U.S. flags were waved from every vantage point.

It was U.S. Veterans Day and this meant the waters were heavily crowded with private pleasure craft. A huge flotilla, including fire-boats spouting high colorful water jets and with crowds of the local residents out on just about anything that could float, flocked together to escort Allure to her Port Everglades berth.

Two days later, off the Florida coast, on Saturday, November 13, 2010, at 5:30 p.m., she met her sister Oasis of the Seas for a special photo opportunity of the world's two largest ships together for the first time,

Her naming ceremony service was held November 28, 2010 and for the honor of godmother, Royal Caribbean again moved to create a precedent in maritime history. At the gala ceremony, 3,500 guests packed the Amber theater to be greeted on-screen by none other than the 3-D animated Princess Fiona, star of the DreamWorks Animation's mega hit film series, 'Shrek'.

After a flirtatious greeting with Richard Fain and acceptance of the title of being Allure's godmother, the giant princess karate chopped the button releasing the traditional bottle of champagne across the bows. Even the champagne bottle was special: its label was created by pop artist Romero Britto, who also has an on-board gallery.

The selection of Princess Fiona marked the Allure's claim to the title of being the 'Entertainment Ship' and a new partnership agreement with the DreamWorks Animation film studio was created.

Richard Fain said that as everything about Allure was different and the fact that the ship is wild and wonderful, and that Fiona was royalty: 'so why not!'

As had been done previously with the Oasis, Allure embarked on a special four-night sailing on December 1, 2010 to the cruise line's private beach destination of Labadee prior to making her official inaugural cruise on the fifth of December.

This cruise marked the beginning of a Caribbean itinerary program with her sister ship Oasis that proved so successful that Royal Caribbean was quickly back knocking at the doors of its ship builders. Incredibly, they had decided that they did not need just two biggest ships of the world. They probably needed four!

On December 27, 2012, Royal Caribbean ordered the third Oasis class ship, only this time it was from STX France rather than from the STX Finland shipyard that built the first two ships. This was because the government of Finland couldn't come to an agreement with Royal Caribbean. Some governments are keener to support ship building than others!

However, STX France had already built twelve ships for Royal Caribbean and the team to build the new ship remained largely the same. Many of the key experts involved in the project come from several different countries and were quite accustomed to working in different places.

So, in fact it was basically still the same ship building company and experienced people that cut the first piece of steel on September 23, 2013 and saw the keel laying ceremony take place on May 9, 2014.

At the keel laying ceremony for the third Oasis ship, Richard D Fain, Royal Caribbean's chairman, the company's president, Adam Goldstein and STX France Chief Executive Officer, Laurent Castaing, announced that Royal Caribbean had exercised its option for a fourth Oasis class ship and that steel cutting had begun on February 13 at Harmony's STX shipyard in Saint-Nazaire, France for a 2018 delivery.

This third Oasis class ship, Harmony of the Seas, is slightly bigger than the Allure. This resolved the contentious situation of Allure being an extra two inches longer than Oasis. Harmony is 7 feet longer than Allure so there can be no arguments about slightly different measurements depending on the temperature of the day!

Furthermore, an extra 18 feet was added to the beam (width) of the ship to make her more than 216 feet across. This adds up to an extra 2,418 gross registered tons to bring the total tonnage to 227,700.

So, although only a comparative smidgen bigger, her float out on June 22, 2015 was the signal for Harmony to tell her two sisters to move over as she was now the biggest cruise ship in the world. Her build cost came in at about US$1.35 billion, but her reign as the biggest ship was anticipated to be short lived with her new sister progressing in the shipyard behind her.

This brought about the incredible prospect of having not built just one, but four sister ships, each bigger than any other cruise ship in the world. With just the four ships it meant that on any one day at sea, there could be 33,000 people living aboard an Oasis class ships

Although it was known that in September 2013 Royal Caribbean had

Fort Lauderdale greeting the maiden arrival of Oasis of the Seas.

At the official naming ceremony of Allure of the Seas in Fort Lauderdale are Adam Goldstein, Richard Fain, Princess Fiona and Captain Hernan Zini.

renewed its trademarks for ship names to include Apex of the Seas, Emblem of the Seas and Joy of the Seas. However, the name eventually selected was Symphony of the Seas. At the time of writing, a fifth ship still to be officially named, was ordered. Is is generally being referred to as Oasis 5.

Said Richard D Fain, 'The Oasis class ships shatter preconceived notions of what cruising can be and continue to stand in a category by themselves. With Harmony of the Seas, we are making the most exciting experience at sea even better.'

Harmony has 2,744 passenger staterooms with a capacity of 6,360 passengers, an increase of 64 passengers over the previous ships in the class, as well as 1,197 crew cabins capable of berthing 2,100 crew.

On Harmony the company made some stateroom categories even larger than on Oasis and Allure. The ship also has an expanded adults-only solarium area and three water slides that twist and swirl from high above.

One of these slides, which stands ten stories high above Central Park, spins riders around in a giant champagne bowl. 'Wow! But, personally, no thanks. I would rather head for the Royal Promenade and its bionic bar with its robot bartenders and get my champagne experience there! Robot bartenders? Well, of course, why not? They are ideal for robotic drinkers.

The keel for Royal Caribbean Internationals' fourth Oasis class ship, the Symphony of the Seas, was officially laid on October 29, 2015 at the STX shipyard in St. Nazaire, France. During the ceremony, a 1,000-ton block measuring 32-ft by 154-ft (10 x 47 meters) was lifted by crane into the building dock. She began her maiden voyage on April 21, 2018.

Symphony of the Seas offers 28 more staterooms than her newest sister ship Harmony of the Seas and her water slide is a little taller than Harmony's.

The introduction of the new big ships era put increased demand on the shore facilities at the Port Miami's terminal. In March 2017, Royal Caribbean broke ground with the construction of a new terminal to be named, wait for it: PortMiami Terminal. This is a 170,000-square-foot dock and was scheduled for completion in time for the arrival of Symphony. It is the most innovative cruise facility in the U.S. It has an expected revenue of $500 million a year and will add 4,000 jobs to Miami-Dade County. It is anticipated that Royal Caribbean Cruises will generate at least 1.8 million passenger moves at PortMiami. This represents thirty percent of the port's projected passenger traffic.

The Oasis Sisters

Chapter Six

Anchors Aweigh

Sometimes prospective passengers express a concern that with the ships being so big and carrying so many passengers there could be some congestion problems. But, as explained earlier, the passenger space ratio coupled with a greatly increased number of boarding gangways and elevators ensures that passenger handling is as good as any ship.

Experienced cruisers find that boarding and disembarkation are superbly managed and that everything runs like clockwork. Both embarking and disembarking are amongst the fastest of any of the cruise ships.

From arrival at curbside, checking in, being photographed and badged for your boarding pass and then completing the walk up the gangplank to be on board, can take less than 15 minutes.

If Royal Caribbean can do that for 6000 people, why can't the airlines manage to do the same when they only have a couple of hundred passengers to handle!

And there are many benefits of being on the mega-sized sisters: the different districts to explore, the sheer variety of the entertainment and if you ever do encounter a dreadful bore, you can go the whole trip and never see them again! So, in fact, the very size of an Oasis makes for more privacy.

But if you do want to keep in touch aboard it is easy with your smart phone.

Realizing the importance of social media connectivity, in March 2014, the company broke away from slow speed Internet connections on cruise ships. In a major investment, Royal Caribbean moved to introduce wi-fi fiber speed with satellite reach to give results as good as, or better, than can be obtained on land.

The company installed sophisticated antenna arrays aboard and paired these with a new generation of medium-Earth-orbit satellites floating around nearly 5000 miles above.

These were designed to bring the Internet to emerging countries, but by hooking into this, the new ships can offer blisteringly fast Internet

Photo: © Paul Curtis

connections.

The key to unlocking a land-like experience was reducing satellite latency – the time it takes for something to happen after you hit 'enter.' The breakthrough technology reduces latency from 750 milliseconds to approximately 140 milliseconds. The ship's overall capacity exceeds 500mbps, so that there is enough bandwidth to serve all guests.

Said Royal Caribbean's Adam Goldstein, 'A great vacation today also means keeping friends updated over social media and enjoying downtime with streaming content played on tablets and phones.

'When the nearest cell tower or cable hook-up can be a thousand miles away, matching or exceeding the best on-land service was a tough challenge. We needed real breakthroughs, not just incremental increases.

'This has been achieved and now guests can stream video, Skype with family and friends back home and share their vacation memories through social media.

'We are also dreaming up some other pretty interesting new uses for all this connectivity.'

Royal Caribbean has named its new wi-fi service as 'Voom' and it is now the fastest Internet service on any cruise ship. Harmony of the Seas introduced the fitting of radio-frequency identification (RFID) systems throughout the ship. This uses electromagnetic fields to transfer data automatically from special identifying tags worn on the passenger's wrist.

Wearing one of these, with a mere wave of the wrist a passenger can unlock their stateroom door, make theatre reservations or purchase anything, anywhere on the ship. They are called, inevitably, ' wowbands'. They are certainly more convenient than fumbling around in pockets for easily misplaced room cards.

Royal Caribbean has also made extensive use of technology and logistical skills to speed the disembarkation and boarding process on the weekly turnaround day which typically runs from 6.00am to 4.30pm.

In this time 6000 departing passengers have to be reunited with their baggage in the quayside customs hall and 6000 new passengers have to be opening their cabin doors and discovering their luggage. About 15 minutes after the last passenger has departed, the new ones start arriving.

For the crew, it's a case of all hands-on-deck as the size of this operation is truly staggering. There can be 15,000 pieces of baggage to collect from the cabins and 15,000 new pieces to bring back again. There're more than 3000 new beds to make-up, 2,700 cabins and bathrooms to clean and it all must be

An evening stroll through the entertainment area and you can suddenly find staging popping out from high above carrying full scale entertainment.

Photos: © Paul Curtis

An ice show on Allure.

The showy bright lights above decks contrasts with the scene deep below in the ship's laundry with its giant washing machine.

done before noon. And on every turn around, the grand pianos need tuning!

Royal Caribbean has consulted time and motion experts to achieve maximum efficiency. Adapting experience from the auto industry, the company has a strict system to ensure all rooms are cleaned in the most efficient and fastest way.

First the dirty linen is separated from the towels into separate color identified bags which are placed in the hallways for collection by the ship's laundry. The 190 housekeepers take out the dirty linen and towels and line them up in the hallways in green and red bags as decreed by the efficiency specialists. They are then sent via the I-95 internal highway to the laundry room.

The rooms are then dusted and wiped in a precise order. To fit the new sheets, the cabin attendants pair up, but otherwise they work individually

Meanwhile, deep down in the ship, the laundry is working flat out. Typically, there are 93,000 pounds of laundry to be done. After washing, all the sheets are both ironed and pressed by an automatic machine. However, all the 29,000 towels must be folded by hand.

During turnaround, the ship's I-95 becomes the most important through way. Fork lifts and trucks are run with military precision to avoid any chance of traffic jams or accidents. If only the real I-95 could be so well controlled!

Passengers can choose between riding Harmony of the Seas' giant water slide or visiting the robot staffed bar. Beneath an array of 30 different kinds of spirit and 21 drink mixes, two bionic arms make two cocktails of your choice in just one minute. Shaking, mixing and stirring, the arms are programmed to mimic the graceful moves of Roberto Bolle, principal dancer with the American Ballet Theater. Move over Tom Cruise! The Bionic bar takes 41,600 man hours to make, about the same time as it takes to build 273 custom Lamborghinis. However, unlike the cars, it can make a thousand cocktails a day.

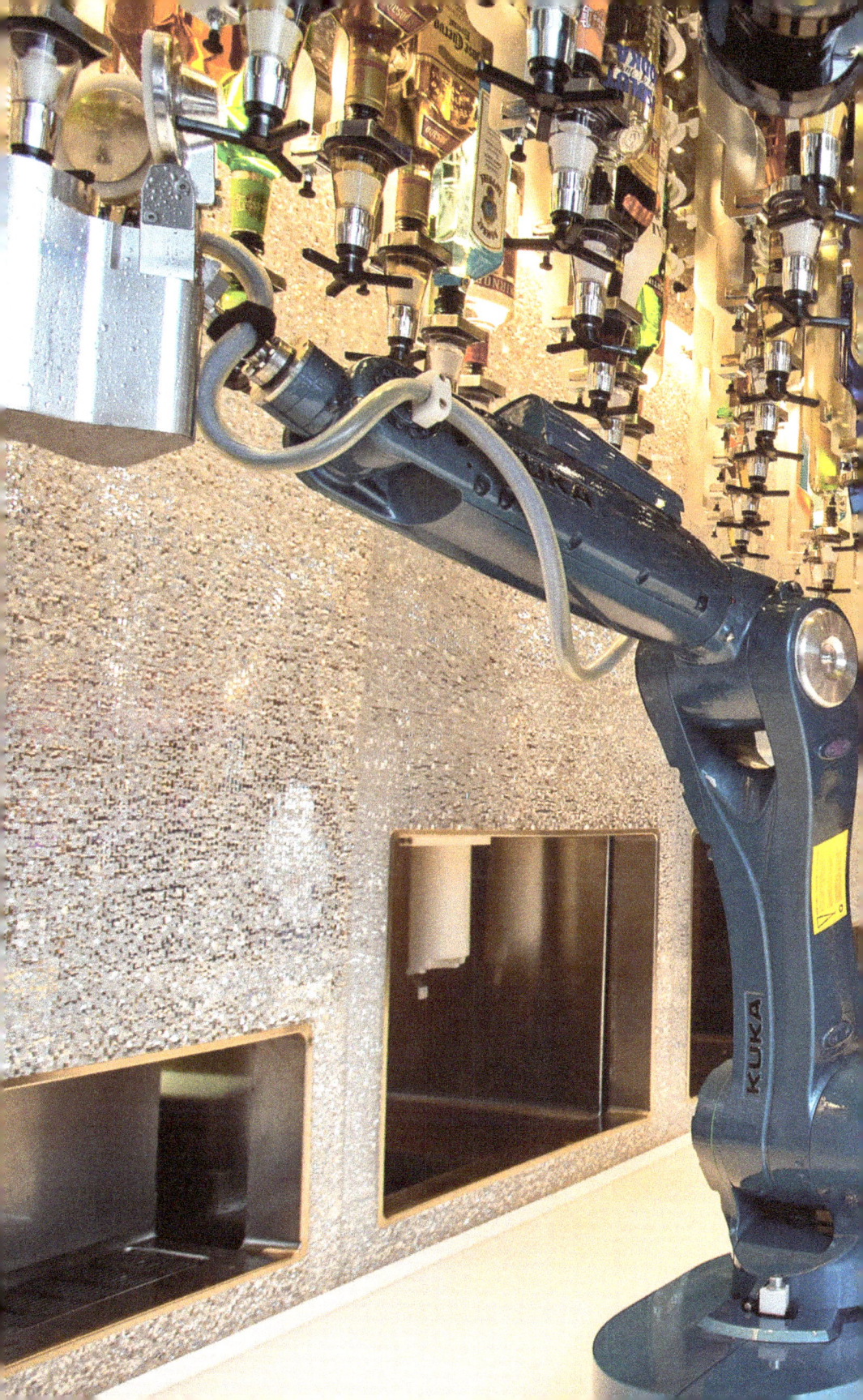

Royal Caribbean has privately owned resorts in Haitti at Lapardee and in the Bahamas at CocoCay.

Allure dominating the landscape at Labadee. Photo: © Paul Curtis

Allure dwarfs dockside buildings.
Photo: © Paul Curtis

Preparing food for the evening meal.
Photo: © Paul Curtis

Offerings from the Cupcake Cupboard.
Photo: © Paul Curtis

Chapter Seven

Food, Food, Glorious Food

In addition to the laundry and luggage, the port turn-around loading traffic includes 1,800 new pallets of supplies. There are the vital 24,000 bottles of beer, 1,400 bottles of champagne and 9,000 soda cans to help produce the 27,000 non-alcoholic drinks served during a typical cruise.

The twenty-four cold-storage rooms are filled with 25,000 pounds of meat, 60,000 eggs, 10,000 pounds of fish and fresh vegetables. This includes 15,000 pounds of potatoes and 9,000 pounds of tomatoes.

The bread has to be baked on-board every day, so in the galleys they have baking machines that can produce 4000 bread rolls an hour. Altogether this is one giant veritable mountain of food to tuck into! So, no passenger is going hungry.

There is a very wide variety of eateries to choose from. Although it varies slightly from ship to ship, there are about 26 places, ranging from Starbucks to exclusive fine dining, such as the 150 Central Park restaurant aboard Allure of the Seas.

As an example of an Oasis ship dining options, Allure's other offerings on the boardwalk you will find Rita's Cantina, with casual indoor and outdoor seating, the Dog House, offering traditional hot dogs; the Boardwalk Bar, with fruit, salads and sandwiches; the Donut Ship for casual snacks; a Johnny Rockets, fifties-style diner with server-entertainers and an Ice Cream Parlor offering a bewildering number of flavors.

On Central Park, there is Giovanni's Table, an Italian trattoria with indoor and alfresco seating; the Park Café, for salads, sandwiches, soups and pastries; the Vintages Wine Bar with tapas and cheeses; and the Chops Grille steakhouse.

In the Pool and Sports Zone, there is the Samba Grill, a Brazilian steakhouse with chiaroscuro; the Solarium Bistro with health-conscious choices; the Wipe-Out Café self-service buffet and the elite Izumi Asian Cuisine restaurant which has a sushi bar and hot-rock cooking.

On the Royal Promenade, you will find Sorrento's Pizzeria; the Café

Promenade has pastries and sandwiches and the Cupcake Cupboard, offering a wide selection of fresh-baked cupcakes.

If you are watching your figure, head for the Vitality at Sea Spa and fitness center's Vitality Café.

These restaurants are in addition to Royal Caribbean's traditional Oasis offerings which include the Adagio Dining Room and the Windjammer Marketplace. The Adagio is the ship's main restaurant and its Art Deco décor runs through three tiers of decks. The Windjammer Marketplace offers great sea views and casual buffet fare for breakfast, lunch and dinner.

Another addition is the Candy Beach sweet shop which offers 72 different types of sweets for sale: enough to keep even the most sweet-toothed passenger happy.

If this all sounds too much, you can simply stay in your stateroom and order room service!

As night draws in, the Allure of the Seas heads out to the Caribbean islands and Mexico. Thousands of residents in the high rise apartments at the mouth of Fort Lauderdale crowd their balconies to cheer every Oasis ship's arrival and departure. There is no doubt that the Oasis ships are the port's favorites. Note the ship's heliport located on the bow. Photo: © Paul Curtis

In the culinary world, being appointed as the main chef aboard an Oasis ship is the pinnacle of achievement

The task is enormous. Although three of the restaurants have their own dedicated chefs, the main chef must manage 24 restaurants and 28 galleys on ten different levels.

The main restaurant has more than 500 tables and can seat more than 3000 guests at any one time.

There are 350 galley staff and 500 waiters. During a normal seven-day cruise they serve 42,000 meals. More than 5000 lobsters are served on a typical cruise. And in the galleys, they have two and half acres of stainless-steel bench tops to wipe down.

Time and motion consultants positioned the waiter stations to ensure that waiters are required to take the least number of steps possible. They are busy: apart from collecting orders and delivering the good, they also keep an eye on such things as cutlery and napkins.

In the main dining room alone, there's 50,000 pieces of cutlery in the main dining room alone and on an average cruise there are more than 60,000 napkins to set and collect.

Ship work is hard on all the staff. The crew members, who can come from more than seventy different countries, work long shifts for seven days a week with only short breaks during the working day. They all eat together in a large canteen where the food is served buffet style.

Three bars for the crew are provided and they go through around a hundred bottles of beer a week, whereas the guests, however, consume 27,000 cocktails a week.

All this requires the making of fifty tons of ice a day to service the ships 37 bars. That's enough ice to sink the Titanic!

Care has been taken to allocate the crew cabins so that the staff are near their work stations. Typically, the stewards stay on-board for four months at a time before taking a two-month shore break. The marine staff work ten weeks on and then take ten weeks off.

A World of Entertainment

With the introduction of the Oasis of the Seas in December 2009, Royal Caribbean set out to provide new standards of entertainment. This included everything from high dive aquatic shows, to comedy acts, parades and show productions of Broadway hits presented to equal the best of Broadway.

Oasis ships have fully staged official Broadway productions of Chicago, Hairspray, Cats, Saturday Night Fever, and Mamma Mia.

A particular effort was made to make the Allure known as the 'entertainment ship.' The entertainment includes dramatic ice shows on the ship's large rink, DreamWorks character productions, music, dance and aerial acrobatics show called Blue Planet and Ocean Aria. These fuses high dive thrills with dramatic aerial choreography.

There are also movies in the cinema, some in 3D, and colorful parades in the Royal Promenade. Add to all this, everything else from jazz performances to a stand-up comedy club. If you get bored on an Oasis ship, you are bored with life!

For the culture vultures, there is the incredible art collection. On board Allure, there is a gallery by Pop artist Romero Britto and 7,000 other works of art displayed around the ship.

Destinations

Royal Caribbean has repeatedly introduced the world's biggest cruise ship. With the five sister ships being the biggest in the world, the closest to come second, or should we say sixth, is another Royal Caribbean cruise ship.

The ships have many different ports of call. The Oasis of the Seas and the Allure of the Seas initially cruised the Eastern and Western Caribbean. Next, their itineraries were varied to try out further afield cruise centers. From bases in Barcelona and Rome, they have cruised the Mediterranean to visit such places as Palma de Mallorca, Marseilles, Florence, Pisa and Naples.

For a destination to host an Oasis size ship, special arrangements with the country to be visited must be made. First off, forget anything that involves passing through the Panama Canal!

With a beam (or width) of 208 feet an Oasis ship is almost double the 'Panamax' size which is the maximum width for a ship to squeeze through the Panama Canal.

For the introduction of the Oasis class ships, Royal Caribbean first had to make special arrangement at its own home port in Fort Lauderdale. At a cost of $75 million the company expanded its home pier to make it the largest in the world.

In popular Caribbean ports such as St. Maarten major improvements were undertaken. At Cozumel, the pier was widened and the approaches to the docks at St. Thomas, St. Maarten and Nassau were also especially dredged.

Royal Caribbean worked in partnership with the Port Authority of Jamaica to complete a new cruise pier at Falmouth and establish new infrastructure. In Haiti, Royal Caribbean worked with its government to construct a 1,300 feet long pier at Labadee, the cruise line's leased private beach destination. In conjunction with the Haitian Government, Royal Caribbean began development of its private beach destination in 2007.

It now boasts such features as beach sun loungers, restaurants, fast-boat tours and the Dragon's Tail Coaster: a high-speed ride through 2,232 feet of tropical flora and rock formations.

The Labadee resort is located sixty miles from the epicenter of the 2010 Haiti earthquake. During the subsequent humanitarian crisis, Royal Caribbean Cruise decided that its best way to support the country was to continue docking cruise ships while delivering relief supplies. The company also donated all proceeds from its visits to help the earthquake victims.

Royal Caribbean also has another privately owned 140-acre island located in the Bahamas' Berry Island chain between Freeport and Nassau. Called CocoCay, this tropical shore bound oasis has white sandy beaches, lush greenery and translucent waters,

Activities include an Aqua Park with a floating sand castle, in-water trampolines and a log roll.

Passengers will never be bored and left with nothing to do on any one of the five Mega Sisters. If you've got nothing else going, you can always get married!

Yes, although a former captain once quipped, 'I can't marry people, but I can separate them.' The captain of the ship can now perform a wedding ceremony and really ensure one trip you will never forget!

All this has made cruising on the Mega Sisters of the Sea the most popular experience afloat. Passengers book up to two years ahead to be on the maiden voyage of an Oasis ship.

Harmony of the Seas in profile.

Seating more than 3000, the main dining room is three decks high.
Photo: © Paul Curtis

In August 2013, Royal Caribbean celebrated its 50 millionth guest onboard its fleet of 21 ships.

The company also owns Celebrity Cruises, Pullmantur, Azamara Club Cruises and CDF Croisières de France, as well as TUI Cruises through a 50 percent joint venture.

Together, these six brands operate a combined total of nearing fifty ships.

They operate diverse itineraries around the world, cruising all seven continents and visiting 490 destinations.

Every day, RCL gets more than 75,000 telephone calls from people interested in booking a trip. It has been voted as the Best Cruise Line Overall for more than a decade and its ships continually win Best Cruise Ship Awards.

Royal Caribbean Cruise Lines and the Oasis mega sisters have truly proved themselves as having mastered their claimed wow factor.

On Harmony of the Seas the spectacular new water slide design sits high above Central Park.

Chapter Eight

Pieces of Eight

You don't need to talk like a pirate, but it does help to know a little liner lingo. Using terms like the front and back of the ships is a bit infra dig. If you really want to show off your nautical knowledge, here's a brief primer.

The Weighty Issue of Tons
First off, let's understand that gross tonnage is all about the volume inside of a ship and not it's actual weight. The gross tonnage of Oasis of the Seas is 225,282.

Her displacement, that's the actual mass of the vessel, is estimated at approximately 100,000 metric tons (110,000 short tons). This is slightly less than that of an American Nimitz-class aircraft carrier.

The difference between 'ton' and 'tonne' is that a 'ton' is a British and American measure, while a 'tonne' is a metric measure.

A 'tonne' is equal to 1,000 kg. In the US it may be referred to as a metric ton.

The British ton, which is also used in other countries that use the Imperial system of weights and measures, is equal to 2,240 pounds or 1,016.047 kg. It is sometimes referred to as the 'long ton', 'weight ton' or 'gross ton'

The North American ton, which is only used in the United States and Canada, is equal to 2,000 pounds or 907.1847 kg. It is sometimes referred to as the 'short ton' or 'net ton'.

The difference dates from the 19th century when the British adapted the avoirdupois system to create the more easily convertible Imperial system. The Americans continued to use the old avoirdupois units.

This also explains why there are differences between other British and

American measures, most notably pints and gallons – and why the English measure their body weight in stone while the Americans use pounds. Maybe it was all a bid by the English to make them feel they weigh less!

These different measures have specific applications in particular fields of industry, commerce or shipping. So as we are dealing here with ships, the term gross tonnage, abbreviated as GT is an index related to a ship's overall internal volume. So, gross tonnage is different from gross register tonnage.

But neither gross tonnage nor gross register tonnage is a measure of the ship's displacement (mass) and should not be confused with terms such as dead-weight tonnage or displacement.

Gross tonnage, along with net tonnage, was adopted by the International Maritime Organization in 1969, and came into force on July 18, 1982. These two measurements replaced gross register tonnage (GRT) and net register tonnage (NRT).

Gross tonnage is calculated not by the weight of the ship but is based on the molded volume of all enclosed spaces of the ship. This is used to determine things such as a ship's manning regulations, safety rules, registration fees, and port dues. The older gross register tonnage was a measure of the volume of only certain enclosed spaces on the ship.

So there you have it. Got it? Phew. Glad we now have that one all cleared up!

Who Was That?

Aboard ship you will notice a variety of officers' uniform insignias. Worn on the sleeve of a jacket or, in tropical waters, on a shirt as an epaulette, the color and the number of stripes tells you just who's who in the zoo.

First check the color of the space between the stripes. If it is white, it signifies that it is a member of the hotel management. If it is purple, you have just spotted an engineer or electrician. Red is a color you hope only to meet socially. It signifies medical. Green is used to indicate communications, or what used to be called radio officers. It's a lot more significant than simple radio these days. Watch out if its bronze, as that means the ship's police or security. And if there is no color at all between the stripes, then that means the wearer is a bona fide deck officer, in charge of all navigational duties.

Okay! So now we come to the stripes. Obviously, the more the better! Four stripes and you have just met one of the real heavies. It could be the head of the hotel staff, the staff captain, or the chief engineer. If the first of the four stripes is double width, you have just met the captain or the most senior man in that department.

Three stripers are also very senior and indicate First Officers, a doctor or a purser, depending on the color in-between the gold stripes.

Two and a half stripes indicate a Senior Second Officer, two stripes a second officer and one and half stripes a Third Officer.

If there is only one stripe then they are only a cadet, forth officer or petty officer. However, they generally have the advantage of being much younger!

Untying Knots

The knot is a unit of speed to cover one nautical mile in one hour. What is a nautical mile? Well, that is 6080.22 feet. To covert to land miles per hour, you multiply the speed in knots by 1.15.

Why such an odd distance? Well, we are not on land but at sea. One nautical mile is one minute of arc on a free circle of the earth. So that begins to make sense. The world is assumed to have a sphere of radius 3959 miles, and by measuring in minutes of arc, it makes it easy to find the distances along great circles. Doesn't it?

It might sound like taking the long way around, but because the earth is not flat, it is actually the shorter route system used by ships to travel long distances. Simple, isn't it?

Measuring Up

The measurement of a ship's length is commonly taken as the length overall (LOA), or the length between perpendiculars (LBP) at the water line. The depth is measured from the keel to the upper continuous deck.

The draft is measured from the keel to the water line of the loaded ship. The beam is the width of the ship. The front of the ship is the bow, the rear is the stern. The starboard side is the right side when facing the front of the ship and the port side is to the left. Now, even on one of the mega sisters, you will never get lost!

Going Continental

For this book, we have mainly tried to stick with the US system of measuring and weighing things. However, if you are wanting to convert some facts to metric, try the following guide lines:
- 1 meter ≈ 3.26 feet
- 1 kilometer ≈ 0.62 miles
- 1 liter ≈ 0.26 gallons
- 1 kilogram ≈ 2.20 pounds

Inside Allures engine room.

Allure of the Seas®
FAST FACTS

REGISTRY: BAHAMAS

BUILT AT: STX EUROPE, TURKU, FINLAND

MAIDEN VOYAGE: DECEMBER 5, 2010

GODMOTHER: PRINCESS FIONA

25,282 GRT

215 FEET WIDE

22 KNOTS CRUISING SPEED

1,187 FEET LONG

30 FEET DRAFT

GUEST DECKS
8 TOTAL DECKS

4 PASSENGER ELEVATORS

4 BOW THRUSTERS WITH **7,500** HORSE POWER EACH

RETAIL
- COACH LUXURY BOUTIQUE
- KATE SPADE NEW YORK
- MICHAEL KORS
- REGALIA IN THE PARK
- PRINCE AND GREENE
- SOLERA
- FOCUS PHOTO GALLERY

5,492 GUESTS (double occupancy) } **6,410** GUESTS (total)

2,384 CREW (international)

🎠 HIGHLIGHTS
- CENTRAL PARK
- AQUATHEATER
- ZIPLINE
- BOARDWALK CAROUSEL

🍽 DINING

COMPLIMENTARY
WINDJAMMER MARKETPLACE
PARK CAFÉ
SOLARIUM BISTRO
WIPE OUT CAFÉ
VITALITY CAFÉ
BOARDWALK DOG HOUSE
SORRENTO'S PIZZERIA
CAFÉ PROMENADE

SPECIALTY
150 CENTRAL PARK
CHOPS GRILLE
GIOVANNI'S TABLE
VINTAGES
IZUMI ASIAN CUISINE
SABOR TAQUERIA
COASTAL KITCHEN
JOHNNY ROCKETS

🍸 BARS & LOUNGES

COMEDY LIVE
BLAZE
JAZZ ON 4
BOLEROS

RISING TIDE
SCHOONER BAR
CHAMPAGNE BAR
SABOR BAR

GLOBE & ATLAS PUB
SOLARIUM BAR
DIAMOND CLUB
DAZZLES

2,752 STATEROOMS
- 1,972 BALCONY
- 254 OUTSIDE
- 526 INTERIOR
- 683 WITH 3RD/4TH BERTHS
- 46 WHEELCHAIR ACCESSIBLE

OTHER VENUES AND AMENITIES
- 2 FLOWRIDERS
- ROCK CLIMBING WALL
- 4 POOLS
- 6 WHIRLPOOLS
- STUDIO B
- ICE SKATING RINK
- SPORTS COURT
- AMBER THEATER
- ON AIR CLUB
- CUPS & SCOOPS
- CONFERENCE ROOMS
- YOUTH ZONE
- VITALITY SPA & FITNESS CENTER
- MEDICAL CENTER

The fact sheet provided to passengers aboard Allure.

Building ships at a prodigious pace, Royal Caribbean makes full use of the block assembly system.

Chapter Nine

RCL Ships Round-Up

OASIS CLASS
Oasis of the Seas
Allure of the Seas
Harmony of the Seas
Symphony of the Seas
Oasis 5 (Yet to be named)

The Oasis class was introduced in 2009. At the time of the launch, each Oasis ship claimed the title of being the biggest cruise ship in the world. Investing seven billion US dollars in five near identical mega ships took the shipping world by surprise. The Oasis class introduced the seven neighborhoods concept to break the ship up into easy identifiable entertainment areas for passengers. Surf wave pools, zip lines flying high over the ship, aquatic theater productions, elaborate Broadway shows, ice-rinks, dodgem cars, and boardwalk carousels make for an overwhelming passenger experience.

OASIS OF THE SEAS

- BUILT: STX Europe, Turku, Finland
- MAIDEN VOYAGE: December 5, 2009
- GRT: 225,282 GRT
- LENGTH: 1,187 feet
- BEAM: 215 feet
- DRAFT: 30 feet
- CRUISING SPEED: 22 knots
- PASSENGERS: 4,074 (Double occupancy: 7,144)
- CREW: 1,500
- TOTAL DECKS: 18 (16 Passenger Decks)
- PASSENGER ELEVATORS: 24
- BOW THRUSTERS: 4 (7,500 horse power each)

ALLURE OF THE SEAS

- BUILT: STX Europe, Turku, Finland
- MAIDEN VOYAGE: December 5, 2010
- GRT: 225,282 GRT
- LENGTH: 1,187 feet
- BEAM: 215 feet
- DRAFT: 30 feet
- CRUISING SPEED: 22 knots
- PASSENGERS: 5,492 (Double occupancy: 6,410)
- CREW: 2,384
- TOTAL DECKS: 18 (16 Passenger Decks)
- PASSENGER ELEVATORS: 24
- BOW THRUSTERS: 4 (4,694 horse power each)

HARMONY OF THE SEAS

- BUILT: STX France, St Nazaire
- MAIDEN VOYAGE: May 29, 2016
- GRT: 226,963 GRT
- LENGTH: 1,118
- BEAM: 215.5 feet
- DRAFT: 30 feet
- CRUISING SPEED: 22 knots
- PASSENGERS: 5,494 (Double occupancy: 6,780)

- CREW: 2,175
- TOTAL DECKS: 18 (16 Passenger Decks)
- PASSENGER ELEVATORS: 24
- BOW THRUSTERS: 4 (7,500 horse power each)

SYMPHONY OF THE SEAS

- BUILT: STX France, St Nazaire
- MAIDEN VOYAGE: April 21, 2018
- GRT: 230,000 GRT
- LENGTH: 1,188 feet
- BEAM: 215.5 feet
- DRAFT: 30 feet
- CRUISING SPEED: 22 knots
- PASSENGERS: 5,494 (Double occupancy: 6,780)
- CREW: 2,175
- TOTAL DECKS: 18 (16 Passenger Decks)
- PASSENGER ELEVATORS: 24
- BOW THRUSTERS: 4 (7,500 horse power each)

Impression of Oasis Five.

OASIS FIVE

BUILDING: STX France, St Nazaire
MAIDEN VOYAGE: Due for completion Spring 2021

Quantum of the Seas.

QUANTUM CLASS

Quantum of the Seas
Anthem of the Seas
Ovation of the Seas

Introduced in 2014, there are three ships in this class. The Quantum of the Seas begun her maiden voyage on November 2, 2014, Anthem of the Seas began her maiden voyage on April 22, 2015 and the Ovation of the Seas on April 17, 2016

Among the new passenger entertainments introduced was The North Star. This is a glass observation capsule that rises more than 300 feet in the air and rotates upwards and over the sides of the ship to provide breathtaking, 360-degree views. The North Sar has been entered into the Guinness Book of Records as the 'Highest Viewing Deck on a Cruise Ship.' The ships also introduced bumper dodgem cars and robot bionic bar tenders.

Power is generated by two 20.5-megawatt ABB Azipod XO propulsion units and two more Quantum Class ships have been ordered with the first due for delivery in 2019 and the second in 2020

Of the current three, two of the ships sail from Asia and the Pacific region. Quantum of the Seas from Beijing (Tianjin), China and Ovation of the Seas from Shanghai (Baoshan) Sydney, Australia; and Singapore. The third, Anthem of the Seas, cruises from Cape Liberty Cruise Port in New York to Bermuda, the Bahamas and the Caribbean. Two more ships are on order. One scheduled for 2019 and the other in 2020.

All three ships are registered at Nassau in the Bahamas and have been built by Meyer Werft, Papenburg, Germany and share the following statistics:

GRT: 168,666 GRT
LENGTH: 1,141 feet
BEAM: 136 feet
DRAFT: 28 feet
CRUISING SPEED: 22 knots
PASSENGERS: 4,180 (Double occupancy: 4,905)
CREW: 1,500
TOTAL DECKS: 18 (16 Passenger Decks)
PASSENGER ELEVATORS: 16
BOW THRUSTERS: 4 (4,694 horse power each

Independence of the Seas.

FREEDOM CLASS

Freedom of the Seas
Liberty of the Seas
Independence of the Seas

Introduced in 2008, there are three ships in this class. The Freedom of the Seas begun her maiden voyage on May 11, 2006, Liberty of the Seas began her maiden voyage on May 9, 2007 and the Independence of the Seas on May 2, 2008.

Among the new passenger entertainments on introduction were pool surf simulators, ice-skating rinks and rock-climbing walls.

Power comes from six Wartsila 46 V12 diesels, each rated at 12.6MW, driving electric generators at 514 rpm. Total engine output is 75,600kW. The ship is fitted with three ABB Azipod electric propulsion units, two of them azimuthing and one central fixed unit. Each pod can deliver 14MW of thrust power.

The number of passengers carried marginally decreased in the later ships.

All three ships are registered in the Bahamas and were built in Turku, Finland by Masa/Aktar Yards.

GRT: 154.407 GRT
LENGTH: 1,112 feet
BEAM: 185 feet
DRAFT: 28 feet
CRUISING SPEED: 21.6 knots
PASSENGERS: 4,960 (Double occupancy:3,782)
CREW: 1,360
TOTAL DECKS: 15 (14 Passenger Decks)
PASSENGER ELEVATORS: 14
BOW THRUSTERS: 4

Voyager of the Seas.

VOYAGER CLASS

Voyager of the Seas
Explorer of the Seas
Adventure of the Seas
Navigator of the Seas
Mariner of the Seas

Introduced in 2014, there are five ships in this class. The Voyager of the Seas began her maiden voyage on November 21,1999. Explorer of the Seas began on October 28, 2000, Adventure of the Seas on November 18, 2001, Navigator on December 14, 2002 and Mariner of the Seas on November 16, 2003.

Among the new passenger entertainments introduced was the first-ever ice rink at sea.

The ships use three 14,000 kW (18,800 horse power) at 145 rpm each. The center propeller is a pushing on–azimuthing Fixipod-type and the two wing ones are of pulling-azimuthing–type steering propellers. The ships are all registered in the Bahamas and were built by Kvaemmer Masa-Yards in Turku, Finland.

GRT: 137, 276 GRT (Navigator is 138,279GRT)
LENGTH: 1,020 feet
BEAM: 157.5 feet
DRAFT: 28-29 feet
CRUISING SPEED: 22knots
PASSENGERS: 3,686 (Double occupancy: 3,990)
CREW: 1,185 (Average)
TOTAL DECKS: 15 (14 Passenger Decks)
PASSENGER ELEVATORS: 14
BOW THRUSTERS: 4 (3000 kW each)

Radiance of the Seas.

RADIANCE CLASS

Radiance of the Seas
Brilliance of the Seas
Serenade of the Seas
Jewel of the Seas

Introduced in 2001, there are four ships in this class. The Radiance of the Seas began her maiden voyage on April 7, 2001, Brilliance of the Seas began on July 15, 2002, Serenade of the Seas on August 25, 2003 and Jewel of the

Seas on May 8, 2004.

The ships have rock climbing walls and mini-golf but are more notable for their extensive use of glass, even in the elevators, some of which face out to the sea.

The ships are powered by 2 twenty-five-megawatt smokeless gas turbines and are propelled by two 20,000kW Azipod thrusters with a 360° rotation. The center propeller is a pushing on–azimuthing Fixipod-type and two wing pulling-azimuthing–type steering propellers. The ships are all registered in the Bahamas and were built at Meyer Weft Yard, Papenburg in Germany.

GRT: 90,090 GRT
LENGTH: 962 feet
BEAM: 106 feet
DRAFT: 28 feet
CRUISING SPEED: 25 knots
PASSENGERS: 2,143 (Double: 2,440 /Jewel is 2,702)
CREW: 894 (Average)
TOTAL DECKS: 13 (12 Passenger Decks)
PASSENGER ELEVATORS: 9
BOW THRUSTERS: 3

Grandeur of the Seas.

VISION CLASS
Grandeur of the Seas
Rhapsody of the Seas
Enchantment of the Seas
Vision of the Seas

Introduced in 2014, there are four ships in this class. The Grandeur of the Seas began her maiden voyage on December 14, 1996. Rhapsody of the Seas began on May 19,1997, Enchantment of the Seas, a few months later, on July 13, 1997 and Vision of the Seas on May 2, 1998.

The first ship in the Vision class was the 1,832-passenger Legend of the Seas, which was sold to the UK's Thomson Cruises in the spring of 2017 and renamed Tui Discovery 2. The 69,130-gross ton ship entered service for Royal Caribbean International in 1995. Thomson Cruises also previously acquired another Vision class ship named Splendour of the Seas which was re-named Tui Discovery.

The Vision Class ships roam the globe: Alaska, the Caribbean and Europe.

The ships use three 14,000 kW engines (18,800 horse power) at 145 rpm each. The center propeller is a pushing on–azimuthing Fixipod-type and the two wing ones are of pulling-azimuthing–type steering propellers. The ships are all registered in the Bahamas.

Grandeur and Enchantment were built at Kvaerner Masa-Yards in Turku, Finland while Rhapsody and Vision were built at Chantiers de L'Atlantique in St. Nazaire, France. Enchantment was lengthened to 989 feet in June 2005.

GRT: 74,136- 78,240
LENGTH: 916 feet
BEAM: 105.6 feet
DRAFT: 25 feet
CRUISING SPEED: 22 knots (Grandeur: 19)
PASSENGERS: 1,992 (Double occupancy: 2,466)
CREW: 760 (Enchantment: 852)
TOTAL DECKS: 12 (11 Passenger Decks)
PASSENGER ELEVATORS: 9
BOW THRUSTERS: 2 plus one stern thruster

The Majesty of the Seas.

SOVEREIGN CLASS

The first ship, the Sovereign of the Seas, was launched in 1988 and was the world's largest passenger ship in service, breaking the record held by the SS Norway (the former transatlantic liner France) However, in 1990, the Norway reclaimed the record by adding two more decks.

Altogether, three ships of the Sovereign class were built and were the first to include a multi-story atrium with glass elevators. They also had one deck with private balcony cabins instead of ocean view cabins. In 1991, a slightly modified sister ship, the Monarch of the Seas, was added. In 1992, the final sister ship, Majesty of the Seas was launched.

During the early 1990's, these ships were among the largest cruise ships afloat.

Sovereign of the Seas and Monarch of the Seas were transferred to the Royal Caribbean International Pullmantur Cruises subsidiary in 2008 and 2013, respectively. However, Royal Caribbean opted to keep Majesty of the Seas and gave her a major overhaul in 2016.

Majesty of the Seas was built at Chantiers De L'Atlantique, St. Nazaire, France and commenced service on April 26,1992

GRT: 74,077 GRT
LENGTH: 880 feet
BEAM: 106 feet
DRAFT: 25 feet
CRUISING SPEED: 18 knots
PASSENGERS: 2,350 (Double occupancy: 2,767
CREW: 912
TOTAL DECKS: 12 (11 Passenger Decks)
PASSENGER ELEVATORS: 11
BOW THRUSTERS: 2

Empress of the Seas.

EMPRESS CLASS

Introduced in 1990, the Empress of the Seas was originally named Nordic Empress. After a massive overhaul of the company's ships at the turn of the century, the ship was renamed with the 'of the Seas' tag to match the rest of the company fleet.

In March 2008, the Empress of the Seas was transferred to the Royal Caribbean International subsidiary Pullmantur Cruises. However, inn October 2015, the Empress of the Seas returned to Royal Caribbean.

The ship was built at Chantiers De L'Atlantique, St. Nazaire, France.
GRT: 48,563 GRT
LENGTH: 692 feet
BEAM: 100 feet
DRAFT: 25 feet
CRUISING SPEED: 19.5 knots
PASSENGERS: 1,602 (Double occupancy: 2,270)
CREW: 688
TOTAL DECKS: 11 (9 Passenger Decks)
PASSENGER ELEVATORS: 7
BOW THRUSTERS: 2

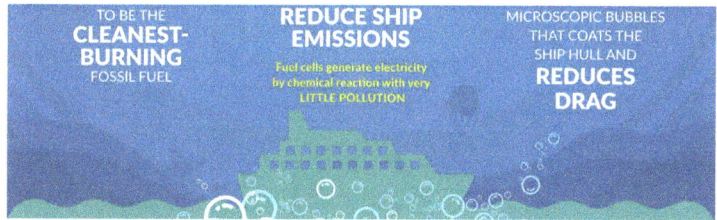

ICON CLASS

Royal Caribbean Cruises and the Meyer Turku shipyard signed a memorandum of agreement for two next-generation cruise ship orders to be delivered in 2022 and 2024. The around 200,000 gross ton large cruise ships are built under the project name Icon and will mark the beginning of a new generation of LNG powered cruise ships with an extensive application of fuel cells for power generation. Smaller than the Oasis class but bigger than the Quantum class, the new ships will accommodate approximately 5,000 passengers.

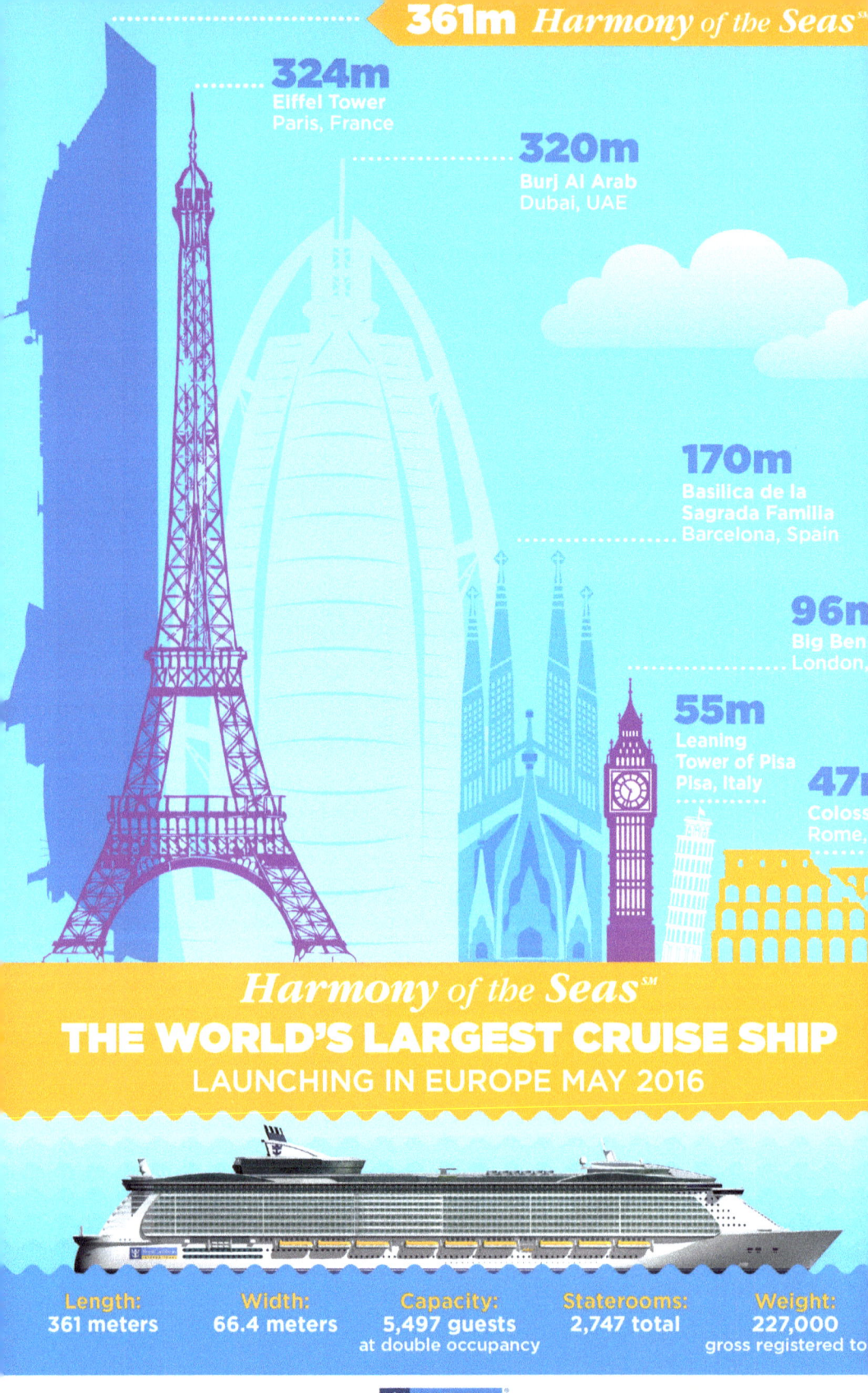

Photo: © Paul Curtis

About the Author
Paul Curtis

Born in Cornwall, UK, Paul began contributing photos and articles to newspapers and magazines while still at school. He quickly became recognized for his yacht racing photos in magazines.

Before he turned twenty, he took a job aboard a cruise ship as a photographer. For the next six years, Paul mostly worked out of New York sailing on ten different ships and covered most of the world's cruising grounds.

Towards the end of his sea-going time, he abandoned his camera for the microphone and worked as an entertainment officer aboard the original Queen Mary, now preserved at Long Beach, California.

Following the Mary's withdrawal from service, Paul moved to Australia. Here he entered the business world before returning to writing and eventually, with his wife Margaret, establishing a magazine publishing company.

He is also the author of the books He is also the author of the books High Tea on the Cunard Queens – a Light Hearted look at life aboard Cunard's Royal Family of Ships, Pacific Princess-the Love Boat and a History of Professional Photography in Australia.

Paul welcomes reader's comments on this book, cruise ships in general and on photography and he can be contacted by email at paul@paulcurtis.com.au

By the Same Author

- High Tea on the Cunard Queens – A Light-Hearted Look at Life on Cunard's Royal Family of Ships
- Pacific Princess - The Love Boat
- A History of Professional Photography in Australia

www.ingramcontent.com/pod-product-compliance
Lightning Source LLC
Chambersburg PA
CBHW040325300426
44112CB00021B/2875